STICKING
TOGETHER

STICKING TOGETHER

The Israeli Experiment in Pluralism

Yaakov Kop
Robert E. Litan

A joint research project of
the Brookings Institution and
the Center for Social Policy Studies in Israel

BROOKINGS INSTITUTION PRESS
Washington, D.C.

Library of Congress Cataloging-in-Publication data

Kop, Yaakov
Sticking together : the Israeli experiment in pluralism / Yaakov Kop
and Robert E. Litan.
p. cm.
Includes bibliographical references (p.) and index.
ISBN 0-8157-0226-4 (cloth : alk. paper)
1. Israel—Social conditions. 2. Israel—Civilization. 3.
Israel—Ethnic relations. 4. Social integration—Israel. 5.
Multiculturalism—Israel. 6. Pluralism (Social sciences) 7. National
characteristics, Israeli. 8. Jews—Israel—Identity. 9. Palestinian
Arabs—Israel—Ethnic identity. 10. Arab-Israeli conflict. I. Litan,
Robert E., 1950– . II. Title.
DS126.5 .L59 2002
956.94—dc21   2001006574

9 8 7 6 5 4 3 2 1

The paper used in this publication meets minimum requirements of the
American National Standard for Information Sciences—Permanence of
Paper for Printed Library Materials: ANSI Z39.48-1992.

Typeset in Sabon

Composition by Cynthia Stock
Silver Spring, Maryland

Printed by R. R. Donnelley and Sons
Harrisonburg, Virginia

Foreword

MODERN ISRAEL WAS founded as a Jewish state, amid the near devastation of the Jewish people in the Holocaust of World War II. In the half century since then, approximately 6 million people, initially sharing little more than their religion, have built a once-barren land into a significant economic and military power, both feared and resented by its Arab neighbors in the volatile Middle East.

The Jewish state was established in 1948 on land previously administered by the British government under a mandate from the League of Nations (later replaced by the United Nations—UN). The UN recommended creating two states out of the former British Mandate, a Jewish state and an Arab state. Arab countries in the region rejected the UN recommendation and attacked Israel in May 1948, immediately after it claimed statehood. Jordan ruled the portion of the land that was meant to be an Arab country until 1967, when it was occupied by Israel following the Six-Day War.

At this writing, Israelis and Arabs continue to struggle over the borders of a Palestinian state. The issue is highly problematic for both sides. It appeared near resolution in the summer of 2000, but with the renewed cycle of violence that started in September of that year, the ongoing Israeli-Palestinian dispute is Israel's most visible reality for most of the world.

The authors of this book, Yaakov Kop and Robert Litan, an Israeli and an American, step outside this ongoing controversy to take a closer look at the major challenges confronting Israel within its own borders, regardless of whether and how the issues relating to the Palestinian Arab population are resolved. These challenges, which are well known to Israelis but relatively little known outside the country, are formidable. They turn largely on how Israel comes to grips with at least four major schisms within society: between immigrants of different generations, between Israeli Jews and Arabs, between secular and religious Israelis, and between Israeli Jews of different ethnic backgrounds. To be sure, other nations face similar challenges in dealing with highly diverse populations, but rarely do these divisions have such a profound influence on the overall fabric of their societies.

The authors find it remarkable that Israel so far has successfully maintained social cohesion in the face of these schisms, while providing increasing economic opportunities for many of its citizens. Israel now has an advanced economy, is militarily strong, and has a vital pluralistic society.

What means has Israel used to pursue its broad social policy of pluralism? Can they be counted on to be as successful in the future as in the past? And, if not, what does Israel need to do to keep its divisions from widening and to sustain a minimum of tolerance toward various groups? Does the Israeli experience provide lessons for other pluralistic countries, with perhaps less intense challenges?

These are among the difficult questions that Kop and Litan take up in this book. Kop is director of the Center for Social Policy Studies in Jerusalem, Israel. Litan is vice president and director of Economic Studies at the Brookings Institution, where he also holds the Cabot Family Chair in Economics.

This book grew out of a project initiated by both institutions, originally with the participation of scholars from the Australian National University. The initial intention was to prepare a comparative study on all three countries—Australia, Israel, and the United States—and to address the lessons that each of these highly pluralistic societies holds for the others and perhaps for other nations in their efforts to grapple with the challenges and opportunities of having populations from diverse ethnic and racial backgrounds. All three societies have been relatively open to immigration, which makes them natural candidates for comparison. However, with the renewed Palestinian uprising, the conflicts within Israeli society, especially those between Arabs and Jews, became more pronounced. Under the new circumstances, the authors concluded that refocusing the project on the narrower Israeli scene would prove more fruitful in providing lessons— both positive and negative—for other societies struggling with pluralism.

The project began with a two-day seminar at Brookings in 1998. The authors benefited greatly from participants in that seminar. Brookings participants included Henry Aaron, Gary Burtless, Christopher Foreman, William Gale, Carol Graham, Joyce Ladner, Robert Litan, Janet Rothenberg Pack, Isabel Sawhill, Charles Schultze, and Kent Weaver. Robert Gregory and Meng Xiang attended from the Australian National University. The participants from the Center for Social Policy Studies (CSPS) in Israel included Chaim Adler, Arnon Gafny, Yaakov Kop, Seymor Spilerman, Herman Stein, and Jimmy Weinblatt. Following this initial seminar, the CSPS team was enlarged to include Rivka Bar-Yosef, Nachum Blass, Yosef Katan, Moshe Lissak, Dalit Nachshon-Sharon, Motti Regev, Rita Sever, and Dov Shinar. Subsequent to the seminar, the CSPS team prepared an edited volume in Hebrew, *Pluralism in Israel: From Melting Pot to Salad Bowl,* with chapters written by the researchers listed above. The current book draws heavily on the studies included in the CSPS edited volume, complemented by other sources.

The authors cannot emphasize too strongly how indebted they are to the work of the CSPS project team and all of the other participants in the two-day seminar. They also benefited from initial research by Barry Chiswick and extensive follow-up work by Rochelle Stanfield. The authors further wish to thank David Birenbaum, Amitai Etzioni, Martin Indyk, James Lindsay, and an anonymous reader, all of whom reviewed the initial manuscript and provided excellent suggestions for improving it. The authors are especially grateful to S. N. Eizenstadt in Israel, who followed the project closely and provided helpful advice along the way, as well as Moshe Lissak and Chaim Adler, whose contributions went well beyond authoring chapters.

The authors are grateful for the financial support of the Atlantic Philanthropies and to the Center for Social Policy Studies, which is funded mainly by the American Jewish Joint Distribution Committee.

Finally, the authors are extremely grateful to Samara Potter, Marina Kunin, Adam Ognall, David Epstein, Yulia Cogan, and Laura Brass, who provided research assistance; to Alicia Jones for administrative assistance; to Elizabeth Forsyth for editing; to Catherine Theohary for verifying the manuscript; to Tanjam Jacobson for proofreading; and to Enid Zafran for indexing. Nachum Blass was immensely helpful in compiling relevant sources and identifying major demographic trends that are cited in the book.

The authors hope that this book will help all those in Israel who are struggling with the issues discussed here, while providing understanding of these issues for persons outside the country who should find some of the lessons useful for their own societies.

The views expressed here, of course, remain those of the authors alone and should not necessarily be attributed either to those who have helped them throughout this project or to the trustees, officers, and employees of the two institutions with which the authors are affiliated.

MICHAEL H. ARMACOST
President

Washington, D.C.
December 2001

Contents

STICKING
TOGETHER

CHAPTER ONE

Sticking Together: The Challenge and the Opportunity

S INCE ITS BIRTH, the modern state of Israel has attracted international attention far out of proportion to its size. No larger than the state of New Jersey and with a population of about 6 million, Israel is one of the smallest countries in the world. What accounts for the widespread interest in its fate?

One factor is that billions of people around the world consider Israel to be a holy place; Christians, Moslem, and Jews revere Israel as the home of powerful religious symbols: as the birthplace of Jesus, the place from which Mohammed ascended to the heavens, and the land of Israel that God promised to the Jewish people. The future of Israel, and of the Middle East, in which it is geographically situated, is thus of intense, and often personal, interest to much of the world's population.

A second reason is that Israel also has been at the center of much conflict in a region of great geopolitical interest. The modern state, initially composed of less than 700,000 Jewish inhabitants—many of them refugees from the Holocaust—was attacked by its neighbors in 1948, immediately after its creation, and has been involved in three major regional wars since that time. At this writing, the nation is wracked with continuing violence, which began in September 2000 with the Palestinian Al-Aqsa uprising shortly after the failure of peace talks at Camp David. Israel also has been at the center of much attention throughout the world in the wake of the terrorist attack on the United States in September 2001.

We do not set out in this book to review the causes of or attempt to resolve the Palestinian-Israeli dispute, although we deeply hope that a solution eventually will be found and the ongoing bloodshed will cease. We instead focus on the internal challenges that Israel has confronted in its past and will continue to face in the future, however and whenever the current violence abates. Indeed, the violence has temporarily smoothed over tensions within Israeli society, while distracting those outside the country from understanding or appreciating the existence or depth of these divisions.

Israel's internal challenges stem largely from the fact that, unlike other countries, where the vast majority of citizens are native born, the majority of the Israeli population, or their parents, were born in other countries. On the surface, the immigrants appear to share much in common: they all are of the Jewish faith or at least identify themselves as Jews.[1] But in fact the immigrants are highly diverse in their religious practices and in their ethnic and national backgrounds and identities.

After initially attempting to "melt away" much of this diversity, over the past several decades Israel has implicitly, if not explicitly, pursued two experiments in pluralism: one centered on tolerating diversity among the majority Jewish population and the other seeking to accommodate differences between Israeli Arabs and Jews. The first experiment has been more successful than the second, but both have had their peaks and valleys.

We explore here the nature of the differences that have led to these experiments in pluralism, what policies and institutions the country has used to carry them out, what challenges remain for Israel, and what lessons Israel's experience may provide for other countries that already have undertaken or, because of future demographic pressures, will be forced to undertake similar—if less sweeping—experiments. We believe that the contents will interest several sorts of readers. Those who know relatively little about Israel, other than what they may know from religious studies or from the headlines in daily newspapers, will learn some of the complexities of the social challenges the country confronts. Those who are quite familiar with the subject matter will see how what they know may be relevant in another context: as potential lessons for other societies with diverse populations that also face similar, although probably less intense, challenges. Our most ambitious aim is to spark a debate both within and outside Israel about the course nations with diverse populations should follow to sustain healthy pluralistic societies—those where citizens share enough in common to have allegiance to their countries but also have enough confidence not only to tolerate but also to encourage and celebrate their differences.

The topics we address in this book are emotional ones for many. We know this from the few presentations, based on the material that follows, we have made to audiences inside and outside Israel. For this reason, we believe that readers should be aware of our own personal backgrounds and experiences and of potential biases that we may bring to the discussion.

As will become evident throughout the book, we share a bias in favor of pluralism as a governing philosophy for highly diverse societies—a bias born out of our personal experience of living in two pluralistic countries. Professionally, we both are economists, accustomed to thinking about social problems and their solutions in a logical, ordered fashion—an approach, we admit, that is not always well suited to resolving issues where emotions run high. We both are Jewish—one Israeli, the other American. Our religious background gives us a feel for many of the topics we take up in the book, but we also acknowledge that it may raise questions about our objectivity. All we can say is that we endeavor to call things as we see them and leave it to our readers to judge how objective, realistic, or practical we may be.

Finally, readers should be aware of the limits of what we set out to accomplish. After outlining our analysis in chapters 2 through 4, we offer several broad recommendations for both Israel and other countries—notably the United States—for strengthening their societies in light of their significant and growing diversity. We paint our suggestions with a broad brush, in some cases with many details omitted. We do not pretend to be exhaustive. Certainly, others who share our diagnosis may believe that different solutions are appropriate. Others who disagree with our analysis may find our recommendations unnecessary or even counterproductive. But we hope that, at the very least, our arguments will encourage readers and policymakers in highly diverse societies not to take the virtues of pluralism for granted or to ignore the constant need to make the concept work.

Why Israel?

It may seem odd, at first glance, to look to Israel as a source of wisdom on the subject of pluralism. After all, the country is unique, and this uniqueness renders it different from other societies. In particular, while ancient Israel dates from biblical times, the modern state is one of the youngest in the world, founded explicitly as a homeland for Jews around the world. The Jewish character of the country, along with nearly universal compulsory military service, has provided the glue that holds an increasingly fractured society together. But it also puts Israeli society in tension with its commitment to democracy, while drawing a sharp line between Israeli Jews and Israeli Arabs. Israeli Arabs, although they are citizens, live and work largely apart from the mainstream of Israeli society and thus largely feel alienated from it.[2]

As a consequence, Israel has had to confront two challenges from which most other countries have been spared. From its inception, Israel has been surrounded by hostile neighbors, two of whom—Egypt and Jordan—have made (a "cold") peace with the country, while others remain in a state of war, even though under armistice conditions. More ominously, Israel lives under threat of missile attack from Iraq, Syria, and possibly Iran—not an idle concern given that Iraq launched missiles against civilian targets within Israel during the 1991 Persian Gulf War. The international "war on terrorism" launched by the United States in October 2001 arguably has put Israel in an even more precarious situation.

The Arab citizens of Israel have strong and understandable emotional ties with residents of the countries that continue to threaten Israel's existence. Some Israelis fear that the roughly 1 million Arab citizens living within Israel's borders represent a potential fifth column whose anger can be turned on them at any moment. That moment seemed all too real in October 2000, when violent demonstrations broke out among Israeli Arabs sympathizing with the Palestinian Intifada and succeeded in temporarily cutting off a part of northern Israel from the rest of the country.

Second, the growing violence associated with the latest Intifada is also a key threat to Israel's security. Although Israel has struggled to find a way to live peaceably with the Palestinians—many of whom live in the area that is now the Israeli state, while others live outside Israel's formal boundaries under the rule of the Palestinian Authority—for the time being, this effort has failed. The Palestinian population continues to grow rapidly in numbers and lives largely in poverty and formally stateless. By virtue of its military success during the 1967 war, Israel has taken on the unwelcome role of occupier of the Palestinians, a role that it has gradually relinquished, but not abandoned. For much of the 1990s, it appeared that the two sides would arrive at a formula in which Israel would recognize a Palestinian state, while Palestine would formally give up its claims to the territory that is now Israel. Major compromises appeared within Israel itself during this period: many on the political right gave up their claim to a Greater Israel, symbolized perhaps most vividly when one of their leaders, Prime Minister Benjamin Netanyahu, withdrew Israeli forces from Hebron. Many on the left abandoned the seemingly utopian claim of Shimon Peres for a New Middle East. The Al-Aqsa uprising, however, set back hopes for a peaceful resolution of the Palestinian issue, apparently for a long time. In the meantime, much of the world has focused its attention on the Israeli-Palestinian dispute and sees both peoples largely through the prism of the cycle of violence that has continued to play out with deadening regularity.

It is tempting to claim that the ongoing violence between Palestinians and Israelis—coupled with other factors that make Israeli society unique—makes Israel such a special or extreme case that other countries can safely ignore the lessons that the Israeli experiments in pluralism have to offer. Certainly, few nations can match the intensity of the Palestinian-Israeli conflict, augmented by the wider threat from the neighboring Arab countries, although there are disturbing parallels in other parts of the world, including Northern Ireland, the former Yugoslavia, and Rwanda, to name just a few.

But it is a mistake, in our view, for those both inside and outside Israel to view the country solely through the prism of the bitter Israeli-Palestinian dispute. Regardless of how the Israeli-Palestinian issues and the conflict between Israel and the neighboring Arab states play out, over the long run, the future of Israel will be determined as much by how the country deals with the *internal* challenges that we outline here as by how it deals with the Palestinians. Outsiders who know little about Israel other than what they read in the popular press might find this difficult to believe, but that is only because they are likely to be unaware of other divisions— "schisms" we call them here—that run deeply within Israeli society.

Yet it is precisely because of the severity of these divisions that Israel's experiments in pluralism should be instructive to other nations that, in less extreme ways, also are wrestling with their own experiments in pluralism and their own cultural divides: Canada (which has nearly broken apart over the status of Quebec), Australia (with divisions among its own native and immigrant populations, as well as difficulties with its aboriginal population), and of course the United States (with its checkered history of racial relations growing out of the enslavement of earlier generations of today's African Americans and the influx of new immigrants, especially from Latin America and Asia). Japan and much of Europe historically have been more closed to immigrants than Canada, Australia, or the United States, but this is changing because they need immigrants to help support large numbers of retirees. These societies, too, are struggling with the challenges of growing diversity (although to date this is more true of Europe than Japan).

Despite its humble beginnings—Israel was once a poor nation, with relatively little military might—Israel now shares much in common with these other developed countries that are confronting the challenges and opportunities of growing diversity. Israel's gross domestic product per capita today stands at more than $18,000, putting it ahead of most of the newly industrialized countries in Asia—only a short time ago celebrated as the most rapidly growing economies in the world—and just short of average living standards in Western Europe. Israel also stands militarily unchallenged in the Middle East, a long way from its precarious beginnings, when the country was vastly outnumbered in arms and personnel by its hostile neighbors. Indeed, despite its small size—whether measured by population or geography—Israel has a military that ranks with that of most of the other developed nations in the world.

A final reason to look to Israel is that its experiment in "Jewish pluralism"—and to a much lesser extent its experiment in "Jewish-Arab" pluralism—has been remarkably successful given the stresses and circumstances confronting a small country, with a highly diverse population, surrounded by hostile neighbors, and requiring extraordinary military expenditures. Despite these hurdles, Israel has managed to develop a thriving, pluralistic democracy, a strong economy, and a relatively high standard of living for most of its people (even for Israeli Arabs, if one compares them to their Palestinian, Egyptian, and Jordanian neighbors). Israel's success therefore should attract interest from other pluralistic societies confronting less serious, but potentially significant, challenges to continued social cohesion.

Israel's Divisions

Nonetheless, Israel too faces serious challenges to its social cohesion from several divisions within its population. These challenges surfaced to some degree after the Oslo peace process was launched in 1993, a not surprising result since the prospect of a lasting peace with the Palestinians allowed Israelis to turn to other sources of friction among themselves. Concurrently, Israel faced the challenge of absorbing almost 1 million new immigrants from the former Soviet Union. Indeed, in this period Israel experienced much social and political instability.

If the past can be characterized as the struggle by groups at the political periphery against those at the political center (or the elite) to gain "a larger slice of the pie," in the last decade the fight became not merely a dispute over resources but a battle over who defines the center itself. In the process, Israeli politics became stuck in a political stalemate between the two larger parties, Likud and Labor, neither of which had enough outright power to govern without the support of smaller "kingpin" parties. In this environment, a consensus temporarily developed that the way to break the deadlock was to change the political system, first by introducing direct elections for prime minister and then by revoking that act and returning to the prior system of having Parliament choose the nation's leader. The whole experience clearly demonstrated that changes to the electoral system are superficial acts and cannot alter the underlying reality that very deep splits exist within Israeli society.

The Al-Aqsa uprising pushed these divisions to the background—except for the one between Israeli Arabs and Jews—as security threats tend to do. But ultimately, the divisions we examine in the next two chapters cannot be ignored. They are serious and may grow more so unless Israel takes even more measures than it has adopted already—outlined in chapter 4—to ensure social cohesion in the future. We offer some suggestions for meeting this challenge in chapter 5.

As we discuss in greater detail shortly, one set of divisions within the country exists between segments of the Jewish majority: first and older generations of Israelis (immigrants and natives); secular and religious Jews; Jews of different cultural and national backgrounds, so-called Ashkenazim and Sephardim,[3] themselves not homogeneous groups; and wide divisions among Israelis by income that coincide with ethnic and religious differences.[4] How Israel has dealt with these divisions is potentially most relevant to other pluralistic societies, a topic we take up in our concluding chapter.

Israel's other, more dramatic, division is between the Jewish majority, for whom the modern state was founded, and the Arab minority, who lived there before the state was founded and, since its inception, have lived very much apart from other citizens. Here, Israel's experience almost certainly is unique: we are hard-pressed to think of another country where a significant minority has long been viewed as a potential security threat by the majority. Nonetheless, even in dealing with this highly fractious divide, Israel may provide a beacon of hope to countries with much less pressing challenges. After all, security issues aside, Israeli authorities have made at least *some attempt* to integrate Israeli Arabs into the wider society. Nevertheless, Israel will have to make much greater efforts in this regard in the future, however politically difficult such efforts may appear at this time, if it wants to sustain a vibrant pluralistic democracy.

As briefly suggested, the internal divisions Israel faces grow, to a significant extent, out of the fact that like a few other countries around the world—the United States, Canada, and Australia being notable examples—Israel has taken in large numbers of immigrants from many places and backgrounds. Like these other countries, Israel has tried to melt these different people into a cohesive nation and has been more forceful in doing so than other countries. The new arrivals initially came to the country with little other than the clothes on their backs and thus literally were required to start their lives over again in a foreign country. They were instructed in a new language, provided with new jobs, and given shelter. Like raw recruits in the army, in which most of them eventually were required to serve, the new Israelis forged common bonds under circumstances of adversity. In a very real sense, Israel originally was very much a "melting pot" and was relatively successful in that endeavor.

At the same time, however, not everything about a person can be reinvented. People cannot be poured into a mold and easily reshaped into an ideal that the state, or anyone else for that matter, may choose. This is especially true in a democracy, where different opinions are not only tolerated but also encouraged, and in a country where immigrants, even though they may have a common religion (for many by birth only), come from a wide variety of national and ethnic backgrounds. Under these circumstances, no melting pot policy, however bold and imaginative, can remove all of the differences among the new arrivals. Moreover, as the Jewish population has continued to grow, it has posed a direct threat to the Arab minority, reinforcing their second-class status in a society created for and managed by the Jewish majority.

As a result, Israel has slowly abandoned any melting pot objective. Gradually, and often with great difficulty, Israelis have had to learn how to live with, accommodate, and respect the deep differences within its population. To borrow a culinary analogy, Israeli society, much like American society, has become more of a "salad bowl" than a melting pot. One of the country's major domestic challenges, therefore, has been to ensure that at least all Israeli Jews have sufficient things in common—beyond religion, which, as we discuss in the next chapter, can divide as much as it can unite—to maintain social cohesion, while at the same time tolerating their differences. Israel's other internal, and more pressing, challenge is to give Arab citizens enough of a stake in society that they will not revolt and find common cause with Israel's external enemies or aggravate tensions, already at hair-trigger level, with the Palestinians.

The challenges loom larger when one takes a more distant time horizon. What will this young country look like in the years ahead, as it enlarges and ages? Today, Israel has about 5 million Jewish and 1 million Arab citizens. But Jews are growing less rapidly through natural means than Arabs. Moreover, the Russian immigration, which considerably augmented the Jewish population of the country, is more or less at an end. As the violence between Palestinians and Jews continues, Jewish immigration from other source countries does not look promising, while Jewish *emigration* (especially of highly trained Israelis who can easily find work in the West) is likely to grow. Israel confronts a potential demographic bomb threat, one whose fuse was lengthened perhaps by several decades when the former Soviet immigrants arrived, but now is considerably shorter.

Suggestions for Israel

How can Israel cope with these major internal challenges? None of the solutions is easy, and, we suspect, none will succeed that is not controversial at the outset. We nonetheless approach this very sensitive and emotional challenge in chapter 5 by offering a few steps that Israeli society and its leaders might consider taking to keep and strengthen Israel's ongoing experiments in pluralism. We have no illusions that Israeli readers—policymakers in particular—will readily embrace any or all of the ideas we advance. But if they accept our premise—that something more must be done to ensure social cohesion in Israel, for the sake of all its citizens and for social stability—then we hope they also will recognize the need to begin considering some bold measures to address this challenge. At the very least, we hope to stimulate debate on what should be done by taking risks in offering our own, admittedly less than comprehensive, suggestions.

First, as difficult and possibly romantic as it may seem given the ongoing turmoil between Jews and Palestinians, Israel should take a more accommodating approach toward its large Arab minority, not just in the interest of the Arabs but also in the interest of the Jewish majority itself. Otherwise, any internal security threat that Israel may see from its Arab citizens will grow. In this regard, we recognize that it is easy to prescribe more aggressive policies to rid Israeli society and its legal system of any vestiges of discrimination toward Arabs, but this obviously will be difficult to accomplish by edicts alone—just as it has been for the white majority vis-à-vis the African American minority in the United States. Only as security tensions diminish will hearts and minds further this healing process.

In the meantime, perhaps the best hope exists with the young. One modest effort would be to have Arab children learn Hebrew at much earlier ages than they do now (mostly in high school) and to have Jewish children learn Arabic. On the surface, this suggestion may seem inconsistent with Israel's long-standing insistence that all its citizens learn and use Hebrew. But it simply is not realistic to demand this of the Arab population, now or even perhaps in the distant future. Instead, a more tolerant approach is called for, and one place to begin is to ensure that Arabs and Jews at least understand each other (even though dual-language training may complicate the challenge of teaching all students English as well).

More ambitiously, the Israeli government needs to direct more resources to bringing up the economic infrastructure of the Arab sector to the standards found among Israeli Jews. This will require significant investments in schools, roads, sewage systems, and community centers. The more the economic gap between Arabs and Jews narrows, the greater are the chances that the emotional divisions, which have widened since the Al-Aqsa uprising, can begin to heal.

Among the various schisms within the Israeli Jewish community, addressing the deep split between secular and religious Jews—those who follow a minimum of Jewish religious rituals and those who follow them strictly—is paramount. Although from inside the country this schism may appear to be as intractable a division as the one between Arabs and Jews, the religious-secular divide is one where Israel can learn from pluralistic societies such as the United States, where religious diversity is tolerated, but considerable effort is made to separate religion and state. Although Israel cannot go this far for historical reasons, a useful step would be for the two communities to engage in a modest bargain. Secular Israelis would guarantee continued financial support for religious educational and social service institutions. In return, students graduating from religious schools would fulfill some type of compulsory service—military or civilian—while the religious community would agree to have Jewish law govern the civil affairs of only those who agree to be bound by it (unlike the current situation, where religious law governs the laws of marriage, divorce, and burial for all Israeli Jews). For those who know Israel well, this trade may sound utopian. To an American, it would sound reasonable and sensible.

A society's educational system is another critical vehicle for imparting a minimum amount of shared values to future generations. Israel recently has established two commissions to address a fundamental challenge: should Israeli Jewish children be educated under strict religious law, or should they be educated as future citizens of a Zionist state that is tolerant of all types of Jews, as well as citizens of other faiths? We suggest that the recommendations of both commissions be implemented. Secular schools should place more emphasis on the teaching of Jewish culture and religious practices, while the nation's religious schools (state operated and private) should devote more attention to the teaching of democratic principles and the role of tolerance of diverse viewpoints. Furthermore, to help address Israel's growing socioeconomic disparities, we urge greater reallocation of Israel's educational resources toward schools attended primarily by children from lower-income families.

It may seem out of place for us to suggest modifying Israel's immigration policies, which, as we describe in subsequent chapters, are among the nation's most successful institutions for instilling social cohesiveness. Nonetheless, in our view there is room for improvement in at least two respects.

One controversial issue that we ideally would like to resolve, but do not expect to do so, at least in the short run, concerns Israel's Law of Return, which grants automatic citizenship to all Jews. Of necessity, administration of this law has required determination of "who is a Jew," a decision now made by religious authorities. The current policy has offended many Jews outside (and inside) Israel because Israel's religious leaders have applied rules accepted only by the Orthodox, or the most religious, segment of the Jewish community, putting into question the validity of Jews converted under other rules, primarily outside Israel. In the spirit of separating religion from state, a more "democratic" solution, if the Law of Return is retained, would be to vest the *government* with the authority to decide "who is a Jew"—more precisely, to decide which conversion practices "count"—*for immigration purposes only*. Such a policy would leave to religious authorities the ability to determine "who is Jewish" for religious purposes—for example, who is entitled to be married, divorced, and buried under Jewish law. But immigration rules and their administration are fundamentally social, indeed governmental, functions and are decided everywhere else in the world, to our knowledge, by government bodies. In principle, Israel should be no exception. As a practical matter, however, we recognize that in light of the continued and recent upsurge in political support for Israel's Haredi parties, it is highly unlikely that the current policy will change anytime soon.[5] As long as it does not, this issue will continue to divide Jews inside and outside the country.

A second immigration-related matter on which perhaps greater progress could be made relates to Israel's policy concerning guest workers. In recent years, as tensions with Palestinians have grown, Israel has become ever more dependent on guest workers, who do not have citizenship rights and are poorly integrated with the rest of Israeli society. Guest workers fulfill many jobs requiring manual labor that once were performed by Palestinians. We discuss in chapter 5 four options for addressing this issue, ranging from extending the aggressive absorption policies now in place for Israeli Jews to limiting or even ending the guest worker program entirely.

Israel's compulsory military service requirement—fashioned out of necessity—also has been key to providing some of the "social glue" that has kept Israeli society together. One sticking point, however, has been the exemption granted to youth from Haredi religious communities and to Arab citizens. Because it may not be politically realistic to require Haredi Jews to serve in the army anytime soon, we suggest a more modest step: community service in a civilian capacity, much like the Americorps program in the United States. In principle, we believe the same requirement should apply to Arabs, although we believe more discussion is required to see how well such a policy would be accepted by the Arab community.

We also discuss in chapter 5 the contribution to social tensions of Israel's large and growing income inequality, especially by ethnic group. A more equitable distribution of educational resources is a long-run solution to this problem. In the shorter run, we suggest that macroeconomic policy give greater weight to growth than to containing inflation. Potentially even more significant, we suggest the kind of tax reform that the United States adopted in the 1980s—broadening the income tax base, while lowering the rates. Such reform should improve compliance, raise additional revenue, and enable Israel to reduce its heavy reliance on indirect taxes, which tend to be regressive in nature.

Lessons for Other Pluralistic Societies

Finally, in perhaps the boldest portion of the book, we outline how other societies with diverse populations may be able to learn from the Israeli experience. Here, too, we are fully cognizant of the dangers of extrapolating lessons from one society to other, very different societies. At the same time, as we have already observed, other nations have had (and will continue) to grapple with the twin challenges of ensuring cohesiveness, while allowing and indeed facilitating expressions of ethnic, cultural, and national diversity. Dealing with these challenges may be more difficult as these societies become even more diverse, with greater immigration.

Of course, existing institutions in various countries may be more than adequate to resolve any concerns. The impressive coming together in the United States in the wake of the terrorist attack of September 2001 is just one of many instances where the country has shown a high degree of social cohesion. But precisely because such unifying events may be episodic, driven by crisis, one may wonder whether, in more normal circumstances, existing institutions are sufficient to accomplish the same objective. In chapter 6, we assess contrasting views of the need for additional measures to ensure social cohesion over the long run. Israel's experiences, while extreme, may nonetheless help the United States and possibly other nations to fashion "insurance policies" that can help them to maintain social cohesiveness while accommodating diversity. Indeed, it is possible that the strong sense of national unity prevailing in the United States following the terrorist attack will make it more politically possible in the short run to undertake the kind of suggestions we advance.

One obvious set of lessons can be drawn from Israel's intensive immigrant absorption policies: mandatory language training coupled with economic assistance during some initial transition period after arriving in the country. One key difference between Israel and other nations is that Jewish immigrants automatically become citizens when they enter Israel; in other societies, legal immigrants typically must wait a number of years. Nonetheless, we believe that Israel's general success in absorbing its immigrants should prompt other countries to examine whether their more limited, "sink or swim," approaches to immigrant absorption are appropriate or desirable. At the same time, any efforts to assist immigrants with integration will be politically difficult to implement in other nations unless corresponding efforts are made to assist current citizens with their language instruction and skills training.

Another, and potentially even more controversial, suggestion is for countries that do not have some sort of compulsory service requirement—notably, the United States—to consider adopting one. The requirement we have in mind would be similar to the one we recommend for Israel: an option to serve in either a military or a civilian capacity. The main benefit is that the requirement would bring together individuals from widely different socioeconomic groups during their formative years and, in the process, help to create a stronger sense of national purpose and identity. At the same time, however, a compulsory requirement will be resisted by some on libertarian grounds and by others on economic grounds: the cost of the program (for the government and in forgone earnings for individuals) and the competition between members in any civilian service corps and lower-skilled workers currently in the work force.

These objections notwithstanding, compulsory service has provided a powerful socializing force for Israel throughout its history and equally so for the United States in the past (albeit under wartime conditions). The idea, in our view, therefore deserves much more attention, especially as American society in particular grows more diverse. Ironically, the terrorist attack in September 2001 may make a compulsory service requirement— or an expanded voluntary one, modeled on Americorps—more politically palatable than otherwise would have been the case. That attack awakened in Americans a renewed sense of public spirit that could easily survive once the war on terrorism has been waged. One way to ensure that it does is to require high school graduates to perform some form of public service (or provide much stronger economic incentives for them to do so voluntarily).

One last point, also of particular relevance to the United States, relates to the role of faith-based organizations in delivering social services. As we write this, the Bush administration has proposed and Congress is considering a major initiative in this area. The proposal has sparked considerable controversy within both political parties. Israel's experience has something to teach in this regard because religious institutions, and indeed religiously based political parties, are means by which social services, especially education, are delivered in the country. Israel's experience provides a caution light to those who might elsewhere rely more heavily on religious institutions in the social sphere, since the Haredi and Islamic organizations that deliver these services have used them to strengthen their own influence among their members and, on balance, have contributed to the fragmentation of society. The same may not hold true elsewhere, and we do not cite Israel's experience as a reason not to proceed with something like the initiative that the Bush administration has proposed in the United States. After all, the fact that religion and state are so closely mixed makes Israel much different from the United States. Nonetheless, the Israeli experience at least raises an interesting caution to which Americans might otherwise not be sensitive.

Concluding Thoughts

We have several modest goals in writing this book. One is that we hope to demonstrate to individuals outside Israel who have great interest in the nation and the stability of the entire Middle East that the daily headlines about the ongoing difficulties Israelis are having with the Palestinians are far from the whole story. Israel has much to be proud of in its short history, but it also has had to confront an almost unprecedented set of social, political, security, and economic challenges. The nature of these challenges, the divisions within Israeli society, and Israel's attempts to deal with them should be of intrinsic interest to many readers, or so we hope.

Our second objective is to stimulate a debate within Israel about the need for additional steps that the nation must eventually undertake to deal with the deep divisions between Arabs and Jews and among Jews themselves inside the country, however and whenever the Palestinian issues are resolved. Certainly, the means for enabling Israeli society to "stick together" are available, and many of them have been used with proven success thus far. The critical question is whether, under the mounting stresses that we have outlined here, the Israeli people and their political leaders will muster the political will to enhance their efforts to maintain a well-functioning pluralistic society in the years ahead.

Our final objective is to stimulate debate in countries outside Israel that already have diverse populations or may be headed in that direction in the future—by choice or demographic imperative—on how they can best promote pluralism. This assumes that they are comfortable with this social philosophy, as we are and as are both of our home countries, Israel and the United States.

We expect our primary audience to be non-Israeli readers who are not well versed in the complexities of Israeli society (which is not saying that the book does not contribute to the debate within Israeli society). For these readers, we are opening only a window onto some of the socioeconomic challenges the country faces. As we have said, we do not pretend to cover all of these issues or even to consider in depth the ones we do address and their potential solutions. Our modest hope is to provide enough food for thought to stimulate the interested reader to think hard about the broad challenges that Israel and other pluralistic societies inevitably must confront and resolve and to lead the way toward solutions that will strengthen these societies in the future.

CHAPTER TWO

Israel's
Four Schisms

SRAELI SOCIETY IS marked by its vast diversity. Unlike other countries, which have core populations that, at most, are augmented gradually with immigrants, the majority of Israelis *are* immigrants. The recent immigration wave from the Soviet Union, in particular, brought in roughly 1 million people in less than a decade, expanding Israel's population by almost 20 percent.[1] In relative terms, it is as if the United States were to absorb a population the size of France's over such a short period.

As extraordinary as is the volume of Israel's immigration, so is its diversity. Chapter 3, which among other things describes the source of immigrants by continent, indicates that, although most of the arrivals came from Europe—a result heavily skewed by the recent Russian immigration—more than 40 percent came from other continents.

In such a highly diverse society, even taking account of the common religion of the Jewish majority, it is not surprising that tensions can and do exist among peoples from various countries of origin. What many outside Israel may not appreciate is that other divisions run deeply throughout Israeli society as well. One of these divisions—that between Israeli Jews and Arabs—is, of course, well known. But the other three schisms, as we call them, significantly complicate Israel's politics and stress the cohesiveness of Israeli society:[2]

—Between native Israelis (older then first generation) and immigrants,

—Between secular and religious Jews, and

—Between Israeli Jews of different ethnic backgrounds: Ashkenazim (of European and American origin) and Sephardim (Asian and African origin).

Although the composition of each of these groups is changing constantly, the differences among them not only continue to exist but also have exerted and continue to exert a powerful influence on Israeli society.[3] In this chapter, we try to explain how these divisions have arisen, how they manifest themselves in Israeli society, and how they have affected the course of Israeli politics. We close the chapter with a brief review of Israel's complicated political system, which, in our view, reinforces some of the ethnic and religious divisions within Israeli society and thus complicates the task of maintaining social cohesion.

Jews and Arabs

It is difficult to think of another society where two peoples live side by side, largely peacefully, who once were literally at war with each other. The United States, with its civil war, does not provide a good analogy, since the country was united before it broke apart in the 1860s, only to be reunited after the war. In Israel's case, both Jews and Arabs lived together before the modern state was formed in 1948, but under the rule of other nations: Great Britain, Turkey, and other dominant powers extending back many centuries. Jewish immigrants poured into the country before, during, and after World War II, seeking a homeland from Nazi persecution. The modern state of Israel was formally declared in 1948, following recognition the previous year by the United Nations. The Arabs living inside and outside the new country, who did not welcome the decision, immediately attacked it. The rest, as they say, is history. Israel has become a major economic and military power in the Middle East, while those Arabs and their offspring who remained in the country have lived, as citizens, in an uneasy truce with the Jewish majority ever since.

The relationship between Israeli Arabs and Jews has evolved over time—in some respects favorably and in others less so. For almost the first two decades of the state, until 1966, Israeli Arabs lived under military rule, originally for security reasons.[4] Arab residents were confined to their towns and villages and not allowed to move outside of them, even temporarily, without special permits. The Israeli government also expropriated large areas of land from Arab citizens for development and other purposes.[5] These actions had the obvious effect of chilling relations between the two peoples. They also severely limited the job opportunities open to Arabs, most of whom worked on farms until the 1960s.[6] During this period, Arabs had fewer years of schooling than their Jewish counterparts, a situation that has since been rectified somewhat (and is discussed later in this chapter). Even Arab political life was strongly influenced by the military administration, which helped to establish small Arab parties affiliated with the ruling Labor Party. This did not prevent a sizable minority of Arab citizens from voting for Maki (the Israeli Communist Party).[7]

The circumstances of Arab citizens began to change after 1966, when the military administration was abolished under pressure from a wide, and quite unusual, coalition of left and right opposition parties—over government objection. Almost coincidentally, a year later, following the Six-Day War, the boundaries were obliterated that for nineteen years had separated Arab citizens living in Israel from those living in the neighboring occupied territories (beyond the "Green Line"). Thus people who were separated in 1948 by the Green Line were able to renew their ties with each other in a way that was impossible before then.

The change in the status of Israeli Arabs in 1966 precipitated a gradual rapprochement between Arab and Jewish citizens, although the elimination of travel restrictions across the Green Line concurrently strengthened Arab national consciousness throughout both Israel and the occupied territories. At the same time, once they were freed of military rule, Israeli Arabs began moving out of agriculture and into jobs in manufacturing, construction, and other occupations. This shift in job opportunities necessarily led Arabs to parts of Israel where Jews lived and worked.[8] Greater mobility, in turn, led to rising incomes and living standards (although these have remained well below the average for Israeli Jews). In addition, growing numbers of Arab citizens enrolled in universities, completed undergraduate studies, and, in a minority of cases, finished master's and doctoral degrees.[9] Unlike their Jewish classmates, however, Arab graduates found it difficult to gain employment that measured up to their credentials, especially in the public sector. For this reason, some Arabs found positions in other domains. Many also became professionals—lawyers, doctors, and businessmen—and served the population in their own sector. Nonetheless, high proportions of Arabs remained employed as blue-collar workers, while some founded their own small businesses.

Although there was some mixing of Arabs and Jews in commercial activity, even more so over time, Arabs and Jews remained very much apart in their social and cultural affairs. As a result, the two peoples have been effectively segregated from one another, and as political tensions have flared between Israel and its Palestinian neighbors, relations between many Jews and Arabs within Israel have grown more hostile.

The attitudes of Arabs toward Jews largely mirror those of Jews toward Arabs, with certain differences that trace to the Arabs' status as a minority. Young people in both communities hold more extreme views than their parents. One may infer a similar attitude from the political makeup of Arab college students, as reflected, for example, in the results of elections for Arab student committees.

The years since 1992 have marked a different stage in the status of the Israeli Arab population, which continues to rise and to benefit from a perceptible improvement in the physical infrastructure in large villages, some of which have attained the higher municipal status of cities: Umm al-Fahm (population 32,000), Tira (17,000), Sakhnin (20,000), Rahat (26,000), and Shifr-'Amr (26,000).[10] Still, Israeli Arabs have a significantly lower average standard of living than other Israelis. Many more of them live below the poverty line and are unemployed than is true for Israeli Jews. Arab towns, on average, developmentally still lag well behind the national average.

Not surprisingly, therefore, separate Arab political parties have grown in strength. Although their electoral representation in the Knesset has not increased substantially, the Arab parties have been successful in thwarting the formation of rightest governments in Israel. Indeed, the Rabin government managed to pass the Oslo agreements in the Knesset by relying, in part, on the votes of Arab members. In this sense, Arabs and their elected representatives are no longer marginal players in the country's political decisionmaking process; they are critical voting blocs of importance in the continuing struggle for power between the two large party blocs, Likud and Labor. This was especially evident during the relatively brief period when Israel introduced direct election of its prime minister in the 1990s. The fact that many Arabs chose to place white (blank) slips in their voting envelopes helped to defeat Shimon Peres (in his campaign against Benjamin Netanyahu) in 1996.

Although the economic position of the Arab population improved during the tenure of the Rabin government, the gap with the rest of the Israeli population still has not materially closed. As a result, Arab demands for full equality have been rising and were attracting more respect, until September 2000, when Palestinians revolted in their Al-Aqsa uprising (following Ariel Sharon's controversial visit to the Temple Mount).[11] For a combination of reasons—some have alleged long-standing Arab frustration with their own economic plight, but more likely out of sympathy with the Palestinian cause—large numbers of Israeli Arabs also resorted to violence, confirming the worst fears of some Israelis about having a fifth column in their midst. The future course of Jewish-Arab relations is hard to chart, but it is difficult to be optimistic. We nonetheless offer in chapter 5 some recommendations for improving Arab-Israeli relations, which we hope may prove to be more politically practical at some point than is the case at the current time.

Schisms among Israeli Jews

Much less recognized outside Israel are the deep, and increasingly divisive, splits among Israeli Jews along several dimensions. These divisions arise, to a significant extent, from the diverse body of immigrants who have formed the nation. They also have deepened as a result of natural causes: differential rates of population growth (which we review in the next chapter) and economic development within different groups. To those not familiar with the internal workings of Israeli society, such a statement may sound extreme. But we ask you to bear with us as we describe three of the most important divisions and then to draw your own conclusions.

Natives and Immigrants

Between 1947 and 1998, Israel's population (Jews and Arabs) grew from approximately 800,000 to 6 million, a seven-and-a-half-fold expansion. Clearly, an increase of this magnitude is too large to be explained by new births alone and, in fact, one other powerful force has been at work: immigration. As discussed in more detail in the next chapter, the gross total of immigrants—2.7 million—accounted for a little more than half of the increase in Israel's population during this period. The net number of immigrants—the gross total minus emigrants—of about 2 million represented a little more than 40 percent of the change in population.

Significant differences in immigration patterns have occurred over time and affected social and economic developments.[12] During the early years of the state, when population increased rapidly on account of the post–World War II immigration and after an economically and emotionally devastating War of Independence, Israelis faced tough economic times. Compounding the difficulties, most of the immigrants had to overcome their own personal hardships and traumas; many had survived the Holocaust, while others had fled from Arab countries that were at war with Israel. In sheer numbers, immigration trailed off in the 1970s and 1980s, but picked up dramatically in the 1990s with the immigration of individuals and families from the former Soviet Union and, to a much lesser extent, Ethiopia.

Israel does much—probably more than any other country—to assist its immigrants and to ensure that they will integrate into Israeli society. They are taught Hebrew, subsidized while they do so, and aided in finding a job. The immigration absorption process has its faults, however, as is discussed in chapter 4, and many recent arrivals in particular have been absorbed in a different manner than prior generations. For example, the Soviet immigrants, who numbered roughly 800,000 during the 1990s, were treated better than earlier generations of newcomers. This is especially true in comparison with those who arrived in the 1950s, when the economy was weak and the standard of living was low.[13] Nonetheless, many of the highly educated Russians have not been able to find jobs that make use of their advanced skills. After five years in Israel, only half of scientific and academic workers who immigrated in 1990–91 were occupied in their profession or in a related field; only 30 percent of engineers were employed as such.[14]

In part for this reason, and probably also because relatively few Soviet immigrants initially had traditional Jewish backgrounds, many of the individuals and families who arrived in the 1990s have been less motivated to integrate into Israeli society than their predecessors who arrived two decades before. Neighborhoods with significant Russian populations have burgeoned around the country, while two parties representing the interests of the more recent Russian immigrants now have seats in the Knesset and the cabinet. There are newspapers, schools, and cultural events aimed at Russian-speaking immigrants. Nevertheless, many Russians have been gradually integrating into the rest of Israeli society. Towns in which Russian immigrants have concentrated, such as Ashdod, have been transformed socially, economically, and politically by their new population. One phenomenon has been the number of shops and services catering primarily to a Russian audience. Russian immigrants also have gained much political influence within these towns. Like earlier Sephardi immigrants, many Russians, through moving into positions of power on the municipal level, have found entry points into the national political system.

Ethiopian immigrants have posed different problems for a country that otherwise is white, considerably more educated, and economically more advanced than the new arrivals. Ethiopians came initially in the mid-1980s and in another wave in the early 1990s. Israeli authorities have provided substantial economic and educational assistance to this population of immigrants but have found it very difficult to integrate them fully into the larger society.

Prior to the Palestinian Intifida of the late 1980s and early 1990s, more than 100,000 Palestinians entered Israel daily for work. Successive Israeli governments and employers have since reduced the country's dependence on Palestinians for manual labor and replaced many of them with "guest workers" (or *gastarbeiter*) from other countries, notably Thailand, the Philippines, and Romania. This policy has created its own set of problems, however, because Israel so far has made little or no effort to absorb its guest workers, whose numbers are thought to exceed 200,000, into the rest of society.[15] These individuals live apart from other Israelis (either Jews or Arabs), often in crowded housing conditions, and have substantially lower standards of living than Israeli citizens. Moreover, because the guest workers are not Jewish, it is difficult for them to qualify for citizenship. As the numbers of guest workers mount and many remain in the country (often illegally), these disparities in economic and living conditions surely will become a source of greater tensions in the future.[16]

Religious Differences

While the sharp differences between Jews and Arabs are well known throughout the world, many non-Israelis may be surprised to learn of the increasingly sharp religious divisions among Jews themselves. Israel was founded as a homeland for Jews, and key features of civil law—marriage, divorce, and burial—are governed by religious norms.[17] Yet the majority of Jewish Israelis are not religious in the sense of regularly observing Jewish rituals, such as the laws of the Sabbath and Jewish dietary restrictions.[18] Many Russian immigrants are not Jewish at all, having entered the country as the non-Jewish spouses or children of intermarried, secular couples, while others who were born Jewish came to Israel with little or no training in the ritual aspects of the Jewish religion (although some immigrants have since adopted these traditions and practices).

However, a significant minority of Jews regard Israel as a holy place. Thus the modern state has attracted a sizable number of religious Jews, or those who are ritually observant. Many religious Jews belong to what we label here as "the Haredi group," or those religious Jews who wear distinctive clothing and whose male members often do not work, but instead study religious texts throughout the week. Among Haredim, therefore, women often are the breadwinners. Other families are supported by the equivalent of welfare payments from the state and charitable contributions. Because they tend to have more children than other Jews (and Arabs), Haredim now account for about 10 percent of Israel's population, a share that has been growing and may continue to increase over time.[19] In the country's capital, Jerusalem, Haredi Jews represent about a quarter of the residents, and if recent trends continue, they may one day dominate the Jewish part of Jerusalem.[20]

The broader religious-secular divide in the country is expressed in several ways. In the political realm, many religious Jews tend to participate and to vote in distinct religious parties, which collectively in 1999 captured an all-time high of twenty-seven of the 120 seats in the Knesset.[21] For education, religious families place their children in separate schools, either in those administered by the state's religious school system or in independently run Haredi schools that are not controlled by the state but are financially supported by government funds. The religious parties have succeeded in enacting laws to mandate certain Jewish practices, such as restrictions on public transportation and entertainment on the Sabbath, that are applicable to the Jewish population as a whole (however religious the individual Jew may be). So far, only the northern city of Haifa has been excluded from this ban on public transportation. Many Haredim also are legally exempt from military service, which arouses strong resentment from many secular Jews.[22] Another source of resentment among the secular community is the fact, just noted, that many Haredi males do not participate in the labor force but instead continue their religious studies through adulthood, receiving state support for doing so. One political party, the Shinui Party, won six seats in the Knesset in 1999 campaigning on a slogan aimed at keeping the Haredim from "taking over the country." Meanwhile, for their part, many Haredim are offended by the secular nature of much of the country, especially rulings by Israel's Supreme Court that intervene in decisions made by the religious authorities and their courts.[23]

Perhaps one of the more contentious issues that divide secular and religious Jews is the question "Who is a Jew?" The issue is important because the Law of Return, enacted by the Knesset in 1950, allows Jews from any country automatically to become citizens of Israel.[24] The original Law of Return, however, did not clearly define what it means to be a "Jew" for the purposes of the automatic granting of citizenship. In 1970, the law was amended to entitle any Jew, as well as his or her child or grandchild or spouse, to all rights of immigration and citizenship.[25] That same amendment also defined a Jew as a person "born to a Jewish mother or who has converted" from another faith. Much controversy has surrounded the question of who decides what is a lawful conversion to Judaism. The religious parties demand that all rules of conversion solely follow Orthodox Jewish law (as opposed to definitions proposed by Reform and Conservative movements within Judaism) and, furthermore, that a conversion only be recognized if performed by the Orthodox rabbinic (religious) bodies.[26] Other segments of the Jewish community disagree with this view.

While this controversy continues to brew, Israeli immigration authorities have stretched the Law of Return for approximately one-quarter of immigrants from the Soviet Union who are not Jewish according to the Orthodox interpretation. Nonetheless, for purposes of marriage, divorce, and burial—matters governed by religious rather than secular authorities—these immigrants are not treated as Jews, which (understandably) has aroused severe resentment among them. Indeed, one flashpoint of anger occurred after the tragic suicide bombing by a Palestinian youth that killed eighteen young Israelis waiting outside a discoteque in Tel Aviv. Virtually all of those killed were Russian in origin, and some were of questionable Jewish heritage. Reportedly, they were initially refused Jewish burial services, which triggered an outburst of protest. In other cases involving Russian immigrants, Jewish religious authorities refused to bury in regular Jewish cemeteries soldiers who died while serving in the army.

Ethnic Divisions

Israel's founding prime minister, David Ben-Gurion, envisioned a country that would be a fusion of exiles, a place where people of different ethnic (and Jewish) backgrounds would be molded into new Israeli citizens. The vision was bold, but the reality has grown into something much different. The initial ethnic division among Jewish immigrants arriving in the land—largely between Ashkenazim (Jews of European-American origin) and Sephardim (Jews of Asian-African origin)—has imposed a long-term imprint on society that is as sharp today as it was more than five decades ago, when modern Israel was founded.[27]

In its first decade, the new state, inexperienced and poor in resources, took in hundreds of thousands of immigrants from highly diverse backgrounds. During this period, the melting pot vision had its strongest hold on the Israeli psyche. All of the key institutions of the state—language training, schooling, and the military—were geared to enable, if not induce, immigrants to shed their past, tradition, heritage, and culture in favor of an Israeli version of Western culture.[28] One of the motives for this approach was the belief in the superiority of Western culture, which led the country's leaders to try to transfer it to all, including newcomers from Asia and Africa.

But the past was not so easily erased. The typical Ashkenazi arriving in Israel during the first mass immigration in the 1950s, brought with him or her more formal education, a smaller family, and more connections to already established citizens than the average Sephardi. These advantages gave Ashkenazim what economists call a "first-mover advantage," one that gradually made its presence felt throughout Israeli society and that continues today. Indeed, for much of the state's existence, Ashkenazim have dominated both the economic and political institutions of the country. Recently, however, the Ashkenazi hold on the country has been weakening, as the presence of persons with Middle Eastern origins has been gaining among the Israeli elite.[29]

Nonetheless, Ashkenazi dominance in the state's early years eventually triggered a Sephardi backlash. The first conspicuous signs appeared as early as 1959, when immigrants from Morrocco staged a violent protest in Wadi Salib, a poor neighborhood in Haifa. About a decade later, the Black Panther protest movement was born in the Musrara slum of Jerusalem. The Sephardi protesters wanted more resources from the state, as well as greater respect from the dominant Ashkenazim, and ultimately turned to the political process to advance their objectives. Initially, Sephardim gave their support to the ruling party but, after continued frustrations, they gradually turned to the main opposition party, the Likud. The 1977 election that resulted in Likud's leader, Menachem Begin, assuming the position of prime minister ratified the strength of the Sephardi political revolt. Known outside Israel for his hard-line military views, Begin's popularity inside the country reflected the profound disappointment of Sephardim with the Ashkenazi-dominated Labor Party, which ignored their economic concerns.[30]

The Ashkenazi-Sephardi political fault line also has a religious dimension. Haredi Sephardim over time have drawn away from their Ashkenazi counterparts as well as from secular Sephardim who have sympathies with the Likud. The Sephardi-Haredi party, Shas, led by a former chief Sephardi rabbi, Ovadia Yosef, is devoted largely to pursuing a religious agenda, centered on state support for Sephardi-Haredi schools.[31] Shas registered its first Knesset seats in 1984 and has attracted growing political support ever since. This momentum is due in part to a general appeal to Sephardi pride and in part to the strength of Sephardi educational institutions and social support systems, which have benefited growing numbers of Israelis, although many, if not most, Shas voters continue to send their children to state schools. In the 1999 parliamentary elections, Shas demonstrated its greatest strength yet, capturing seventeen of the 120 seats in the Israeli Knesset, making it the third-largest party in that body, almost as large as Likud (which captured nineteen seats that year).[32]

The Ashkenazi-Haredi alliance, meanwhile, has been manifested in the Agudath Israel Party. Its members have maintained lives of self-imposed seclusion, and only a few have involved themselves in general public affairs, mainly at the governmental level. Agudath Israel has had strained relations with the religious-Zionist camp, differing over issues of religion and state. In particular, the Ashkenazi Haredim often have supported whichever ruling party was in power in return for state subsidies for their separate systems of education and social services, as well as support for their continued exemption from military service and laws governing public life in ways that are consistent with religions practices (such as restricted commercial operations on the Sabbath).

The 1967 Six-Day War marked a critical turning point for one of the other important political religious parties. Prior to that war, the religious-Zionist camp (also known as the National Religious Party—NRP) aligned closely with the governing Labor Party coalition and shared its views on state security and socioeconomic issues. After the war, a "young guard" within the NRP took a sharply militant turn, opposing any "land-for-peace" arrangements with the Arab countries.[33] The extent of the move away from the Labor Party is illustrated by the NRP's central role in development of the settlement movement in Judea and Samaria (areas captured by Israel from Jordan during the 1967 war). Today, the NRP's major constituency consists of the religious Ashkenazi settlers and their supporters. In the public eye, the party is seen as the settlement movement's political voice.

Over the last decade more and more Sephardi voters left both the Likud and the National Religious Party and gave their allegiance to Shas. This party was instrumental in forming the government under Ehud Barak in 1999, but by February 2001, it had abandoned him, causing an early election, which Ariel Sharon won to become Israel's current prime minister. Together with the rise of the B'Aliyah Party, led by former Soviet political

prisoner Natan Sharansky and one of the two political parties representing the interests of Russian immigrants, the rise of Shas represents a marked
weakening of melting pot politics and instead reinforces the development
of a politics centered on ethnic and religious allegiances.

Both natural population increase and the immigration process have
shifted the ethnic balance from time to time. During Israel's first decade,
the two groups—Ashkenazim and Sephardim—had rough numerical par-
ity. By the second decade, higher birth rates among Sephardim tilted the
balance in their favor, which ultimately led to the Likud's takeover of the
government in 1977. Immigration from the former Soviet Union has since
returned the balance to rough equilibrium.

Evidence of Difference

The abstract distinctions that social scientists draw among peoples are
sometimes best illustrated by looking at how they actually live. Do members of different groups live in homogeneous neighborhoods, or is there
substantial mixing? What are the differences, if any, in their educational
and socioeconomic status? Here we assess the evidence, which highlights
the fact that the schisms just identified are very much reflected in the daily
lives of Israeli citizens.

Residence

The clearest sign of physical separation in Israel is found in the residential location of Jews and Arabs. In the fifty years prior to creation of the
state of Israel, Arabs and Jews lived in separate quarters within a city or in
entirely separate villages and towns. After 1948, Arabs were confined to their
localities for security reasons. Although military oversight has since been
relaxed, residential separation continues. There are a few exceptions, however, such as Tel Aviv and Haifa, of Jewish towns that have Arab minorities.
In these locales, there is at least some degree of residential integration.[34]

Residential clustering also is evident within the Arab and Jewish com-
munities. For example, in Arab localities, members of various religious
subgroups—Christians (the highest-income group among the Arabs),
Muslims, and Druze—tend to coexist separately (with a few exceptions).
Among Jews, ethnic mixing in neighborhoods is much more common.
Even Sephardi Haredim can be found in areas otherwise populated by

secular Jews. This is not the case with Ashkenazi Haredim, who tend to live in well-demarcated neighborhoods.[35]

There is also a significant degree of residential separation among Jews of different ethnicity, corresponding roughly to the split between Ashkenazim and Sephardim, but also heavily influenced by socioeconomic status. Broadly speaking, Ashkenazim dwell in more affluent localities and neighborhoods, while Sephardim heavily populate so-called development towns (new towns created by the government in an effort to disperse the population) and disadvantaged urban neighborhoods. Where Ashkenazim and Sephardim are of relatively equal socioeconomic status—especially upper income—there is much greater residential integration (as is true in other countries).

The immigrants of the 1990s also are gradually mixing with Israeli natives, although significant numbers of Russians cluster together. As one American correspondent has observed, "Newcomers from Russia settle in what have become immigrant quarters of some Israeli cities, shopping in their own stores and reading their own Russian-language press."[36] This differs from residential patterns of earlier years, when official government policy was to direct, in top-down fashion, immigrants into more remote locations, easing their transition with a package of economic benefits. Today, recent immigrants can be found throughout the country, including major urban areas, such as Haifa, Ashdod, Netanya, Beersheva, and Tel Aviv, and several medium and small towns, such as Upper Nazareth, Or Akiva, Karmiel, Sederot, and Ma'a lot.

To be sure, residential clustering—by ethnicity, religion, and income—hardly is unique to Israel. Countries all over the world display similar patterns. Nonetheless, the distinctive residential patterns within Israel broadly reinforce the other sharp divisions among ethnic and religious groups and thus also reinforce the importance of countervailing institutions—notably the Israeli military—in acquainting Israelis, not only in their formative years but (for males) throughout their adult lives, with individuals from much different socioeconomic backgrounds than their own.

Employment and Education

Israeli Arabs and Jews not only live apart but also work apart. Security concerns are one reason. During Israel's first two decades, Arabs were not employed in stable government jobs outside their localities (with some exceptions).[37] Even today, many well-educated Arabs find it difficult to obtain work suitable to their training, a situation also influenced by security reasons (which create barriers for employment in security-sensitive areas). For Jews, the Israeli army not only is the "great equalizer"—bringing together teenagers and adults from different backgrounds—but also provides a social infrastructure and employment network from which many of those who serve benefit throughout their working lives. Because Arabs, in general, are excluded from service in the military for security reasons,[38] they are excluded from this critical vehicle of job networking and thus find themselves looking for work in a largely separate labor market— one whose economic rewards are more limited than those available to Israeli Jews.

One significant feature of the Israeli labor market is not at all unique to the country. As in industrial economies generally, the female participation rate has climbed rapidly over time, to the point where it is nearing that of males (roughly 60 percent). Still, the Jewish female participation rate of 51 percent significantly outpaces that of Arab women (22 percent). Women immigrants from the former Soviet Union have especially high participation rates for several reasons: they were used to working in their home country, they need to supplement their husband's income in Israel, and the percentage of single-parent families is higher than average.

How do all these forces affect the socioeconomic status of members of different groups within Israel? A good starting point is to examine the history of educational attainment of those groups. On this score, there is much that is encouraging. Table 2-1 and figure 2-1 both show that not only has the Israeli population become more educated over time, but also the disparities in educational attainment of different groups in Israel, including Jews and Arabs, have narrowed. Arabs have increased their average educational levels the most over the past thirty years, and, although they continue to lag behind the average years of schooling of Israeli Jews, they are now much closer in median years of schooling to Jews than they were three decades ago.

The obvious question raised by these data is whether the somewhat steady progress toward narrower disparities in educational attainment has translated into a narrowing of occupational and income gaps between the various ethnic and religious groups within Israel. Here, the answer is more complicated and somewhat disturbing.

Table 2-1. Median Years of Schooling and Percentage of Persons Ages Fifteen and Over, by Years of Schooling and Population Group, 1965–99
Percent (except for medians)

Years of schooling and year	Total population	Total Jews	Israel born by father's origin				Asia-Africa born	Europe-America born	Arabs
			Total	Israel	Asia-Africa	Europe-America			
1965									
0–8	56.2	52.9	26.5	n.a.	n.a.	n.a.	74.2	46.8	90.8
13+	9.4	10.3	16.2	n.a.	n.a.	n.a.	3.6	13.3	0.9
Median	8.3	8.6	10.6	n.a.	n.a.	n.a.	6.4	9.3	2.7
1975									
0–8	41.7	37.6	17.0	17.6	27.5	7.2	61.5	37.1	73.7
13+	16.0	17.7	21.5	20.8	7.3	34.7	7.0	22.9	4.5
Median	9.8	10.3	11.1	11.1	10.4	11.9	7.6	10.3	6.5
1985									
0–8	29.3	25.4	9.6	8.7	13.9	4.0	50.7	29.6	53.2
13+	22.1	24.4	27.1	27.8	13.7	45.8	11.2	31.1	8.4
Median	11.2	11.5	12.0	12.0	11.5	12.8	8.9	11.5	8.6
1990									
0–8	25.0	20.3	6.2	4.5	9.2	2.9	47.2	25.3	50.3
13+	25.3	28.2	30.2	30.3	17.6	49.1	13.9	36.2	9.1
Median	11.6	11.9	12.0	12.2	11.8	13.0	9.4	11.9	9.0
1995									
0–8	18.9	15.1	4.6	2.9	6.6	2.4	43.2	17.0	38.7
13+	32.4	36.0	35.7	35.1	24.6	54.1	16.2	46.8	14.2
Median	12.0	12.2	12.4	12.4	12.1	13.5	10.1	12.7	10.2
1999									
0–8	15.8	12.2	3.8	2.8	5.6	2.1	40.6	12.8	33.6
13+	36.7	40.4	40.3	38.6	30.2	57.7	18.8	51.2	19.7
Median	12.2	12.5	12.6	12.5	12.3	13.8	10.5	13.1	10.8

Source: Central Bureau of Statistics, *Statistical Abstract of Israel*, vol. 51 (Jerusalem: Central Bureau of Statistics, 2000).
n.a. Not available.

We begin with occupational data. Table 2-2 reflects the limited employment opportunities available to Arab Israelis, at least through the mid-1990s. Relatively few Arabs work in academic or administrative positions, despite the increasing availability of trained Arab labor for these

Figure 2-1. Median Years of Schooling of Persons Ages Fifteen and Over, Jews by Origin and Arabs, 1965–99

Years of schooling

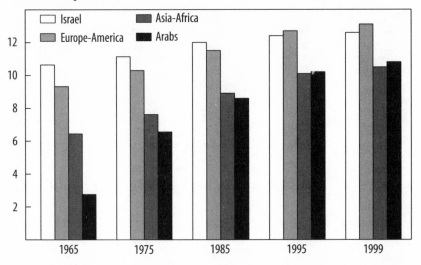

Source: Central Bureau of Statistics, *Statistical Abstract of Israel* (Jerusalem: Central Bureau of Statistics, various years).

positions. Instead, Arabs continue to be concentrated in blue-collar and unskilled positions. Moreover, most of the areas with especially high unemployment rates are Arab localities.

Among Jewish Israelis, there also are marked differences in occupational patterns across ethnic groups. As shown in table 2-3, Ashkenazim continue to be far more represented in the higher-paying and higher-prestige administrative and academic jobs than Sephardim. The reverse is true for blue-collar and unskilled positions. It is encouraging, however, that the gap between the two groups has been narrowing over time. In effect, Sephardim have been moving out of unskilled jobs, while guest workers from Asia and Eastern Europe—and, until the recent uprisings, Palestinians—have been performing this work. The good news is that greater training has improved both the absolute and relative economic positions of Sephardim. More problematic is the fact that Arabs remain concentrated in low-skilled positions, despite their improved training, while the influx of guest workers

Table 2-2. Occupation of Employed Persons, by Population Group, 1961–99
Percent

Occupation and year	Total population	Total Jews	Israel born by father's origin				Asia-Africa born	Europe-America born		Arabs
			Total	Israel	Asia-Africa	Europe-America		Total	1990+	
1961										
Scientific	21.3	26.5	44.0	n.a.	n.a.	n.a.	11.0	31.1	n.a.	5.6
Service	16.5	21.8	11.5	n.a.	n.a.	n.a.	24.6	23.3	n.a.	12.1
Industrial	23.2	19.1	21.7	n.a.	n.a.	n.a.	24.4	14.9	n.a.	70.1
Unskilled	39.0	32.6	22.8	n.a.	n.a.	n.a.	40.4	30.8	n.a.	12.2
1970										
Scientific	32.9	35.2	46.0	n.a.	n.a.	n.a.	19.0	42.0	n.a.	7.3
Service	20.2	20.4	13.6	n.a.	n.a.	n.a.	25.1	20.4	n.a.	18.6
Industrial	22.3	19.3	18.9	n.a.	n.a.	n.a.	24.8	15.4	n.a.	54.4
Unskilled	24.6	25.1	21.5	n.a.	n.a.	n.a.	31.0	22.3	n.a.	19.7
1980										
Scientific	26.4	27.7	33.5	34.5	16.8	46.9	14.3	32.4	n.a.	13.9
Service	37.2	39.1	36.6	39.0	42.4	31.4	43.4	38.3	n.a.	20.2
Industrial	32.1	29.7	28.2	25.5	37.6	20.9	36.7	25.8	n.a.	53.8
Unskilled	4.3	3.4	1.7	1.0	3.1	0.8	5.7	3.5	n.a.	12.2
1990										
Scientific	30.1	32.7	34.2	34.5	20.8	49.4	20.3	40.5	n.a.	13.5
Service	38.6	40.7	40.8	43.8	46.3	33.5	46.1	35.4	n.a.	27.4
Industrial	27.2	24.6	23.4	20.7	30.3	16.4	30.3	21.9	n.a.	49.2
Unskilled	3.0	2.1	1.6	1.1	2.6	0.7	3.3	2.2	n.a.	9.8
1996										
Scientific	31.1	33.7	35.6	39.3	24.1	49.3	22.3	35.7	24.6	14.4
Service	33.8	35.9	39.6	39.3	43.8	33.9	37.7	27.9	24.1	19.8
Industrial	26.5	22.7	19.8	15.9	25.4	14.5	27.9	25.4	34.0	52.3
Unskilled	8.5	7.8	5.0	5.5	6.8	2.3	12.0	11.0	17.3	13.5
1999										
Scientific	33.5	35.8	37.9	40.9	26.3	51.1	24.2	37.0	26.9	18.2
Service	35.3	37.2	40.4	41.3	45.0	33.3	39.8	29.7	28.5	22.9
Industrial	22.9	19.6	17.1	13.2	22.3	12.9	24.5	22.3	28.2	45.2
Unskilled	8.3	7.5	4.7	4.7	6.3	2.6	11.5	11.2	16.3	13.8

Source: Central Bureau of Statistics, *Statistical Abstract of Israel*, vol. 51 (Jerusalem: Central Bureau of Statistics, 2000).
n.a. Not available.

Table 2-3. Makeup of Occupations, by Population Group, 1961–99
Percent

Occupation and year	Total Jews	Israel born by father's origin				Asia-Africa born	Europe-America born	Arabs
		Total	Israel	Asia-Africa	Europe-America			
1961								
Percent in labor force	92	n.a.	n.a.	n.a.	n.a.	n.a.	n.a.	8
Scientific	98	25	n.a.	n.a.	n.a.	13	60	2
Industrial	82	14	n.a.	n.a.	n.a.	34	33	18
Unskilled workers	92	10	n.a.	n.a.	n.a.	37	46	8
1970								
Percent in labor force	88	24	n.a.	n.a.	n.a.	29	35	12
Scientific	97	30	n.a.	n.a.	n.a.	18	49	3
Industrial	79	18	n.a.	n.a.	n.a.	34	27	21
Unskilled workers	92	19	n.a.	n.a.	n.a.	38	35	8
1980								
Percent in labor force	90	35	3	14	17	25	30	10
Scientific	95	43	6	8	28	14	38	5
Industrial	83	30	4	15	10	29	25	17
Unskilled workers	71	13	1	9	3	33	25	29
1990								
Percent in labor force	89	50	9	22	18	20	23	11
Scientific	95	53	8	14	30	13	29	5
Industrial	79	40	6	23	11	21	17	22
Unskilled workers	61	25	3	18	4	21	16	39
1999								
Percent in labor force	87	51	13	23	15	11	25	13
Scientific	93	57	15	17	24	8	28	7
Industrial	74	38	7	21	9	12	24	26
Unskilled workers	79	29	7	17	5	15	34	22

Source: Central Bureau of Statistics, *Statistical Abstract of Israel* (Jerusalem: Central Bureau of Statistics, various years).

n.a. Not available.

who are not citizens, nor likely to be, presents a new and difficult challenge for Israelis intent on maintaining the pluralistic fabric of their society.

Income

Perhaps the key measure of economic progress is the level of income that members of different groups are earning. Here, the Israeli data—which are a bit outdated (because more recent data are not available)—paint a disturbing picture. We report this information because, if anything, income inequality likely has risen over the past several years.

Again, we begin with the Arab-Jewish divide. Table 2-4 illustrates the ethnic and religious makeup of different deciles of the Israeli income distribution over the 1985–98 period. The table indicates that the share of Arabs in the lowest decile in all years (except 1991) exceeded their share in the population as a whole by a factor of about two. Only 1–3 percent of Arabs consistently belonged in the highest decile. The reverse was true for Jews, who collectively were far more represented toward the top of the income distribution than their share of the total population would indicate.

In contrast, among Jews themselves, the data shown in table 2-4 demonstrate some of the encouraging news also reflected in the occupational data. Over time, Sephardi Jews have moved up the income ladder, although the influx of Russian immigrants—which in its early years weighed down the average incomes for Jews of European origin—explains some of the change in the relative Sephardi position. Still, the income mobility of Jews from Sephardi backgrounds, who formerly were less trained than Ashkenazim and often were discriminated against (subtly if not overtly), is a favorable trend and one that should help to ease the tensions that otherwise exist between these two ethnic groups.

The income inequalities in Israel should not detract from the country's generally impressive overall economic performance. As figure 2-2 illustrates, Israel's gross domestic product has grown more rapidly during each of the last three decades than those of the United States and the world as a whole. That this was true in the 1980s is remarkable, since Israeli economic policy during the middle years of the decade was devoted to conquering hyperinflation. Israel's economic performance was especially noteworthy during the 1990s, a decade in which the population expanded more than 20 percent, largely due to the Russian immigration. Israel's

Table 2-4. Urban Households Headed by Employees, by Deciles of Gross Monthly Money Income, 1985–98
Percent

Origin of household head and year	Total	Decile of income			
		Lower	2	3	4
1985					
Jews	95.7	90.8	92.4	93.8	94.9
Continent of birth					
Asia-Africa	29.9	32.9	35.1	38.1	34.5
Europe-America	29.1	26.3	23.6	25.7	22.8
Israel	36.6	31.6	33.6	30.1	37.6
Arabs	4.3	9.2	7.6	6.2	5.1
1990					
Jews	94.1	90.4	89.0	88.9	93.5
Continent of birth					
Asia-Africa	24.8	24.4	23.8	23.6	22.4
Europe-America	24.7	21.3	23.7	21.1	21.6
Israel	44.6	44.7	41.6	44.2	49.6
Arabs	5.9	9.6	11.0	11.1	6.5
1991					
Jews	94.4	96.0	88.9	90.3	91.7
Continent of birth					
Asia-Africa	23.1	22.6	21.8	25.8	27.1
Europe-America	27.2	30.7	23.1	27.7	24.8
Israel	44.0	42.7	43.4	36.6	39.8
Arabs	5.6	4.0	11.1	9.7	8.3
1994					
Jews	94.0	89.4	91.5	91.0	91.5
Continent of birth					
Asia-Africa	17.8	13.2	17.6	15.2	16.0
Europe-America	30.1	38.9	30.6	38.1	29.2
Israel	45.9	37.3	43.3	37.4	45.9
Arabs	6.0	10.6	8.5	9.0	8.5
1998					
Jews	86.5	79.2	74.1	79.0	80.4
Continent of birth					
Asia-Africa	13.2	9.2	11.6	13.2	14.4
Europe-America	28.4	34.1	28.2	29.6	27.8
Israel	44.7	35.8	33.1	36.1	38.0
Arabs	13.5	20.9	25.9	21.0	19.6

Source: Central Bureau of Statistics, *Statistical Abstract of Israel* (Jerusalem: Central Bureau of Statistics, various years).

Decile of income						Origin of household
5	6	7	8	9	Upper	head and year
						1985
94.0	96.6	98.0	98.6	99.0	98.0	Jews
						Continent of birth
29.6	30.9	26.3	30.9	25.1	15.7	Asia-Africa
27.0	27.5	29.2	32.0	38.6	38.5	Europe-America
37.4	38.2	42.5	35.7	35.3	44.3	Israel
6.0	3.4	2.0	1.4	1.0	1.5	Arabs
						1990
91.6	94.8	97.0	97.3	98.8	99.6	Jews
						Continent of birth
25.7	27.1	29.0	26.5	26.7	19.1	Asia-Africa
20.2	23.8	21.6	25.6	31.1	36.5	Europe-America
45.6	43.8	46.7	45.2	41.0	44.0	Israel
8.4	5.2	3.0	2.7	1.2	0.4	Arabs
						1991
94.1	94.1	96.1	95.8	98.4	98.6	Jews
						Continent of birth
28.9	24.0	24.3	22.2	18.0	16.2	Asia-Africa
20.3	26.3	24.6	25.7	31.4	36.9	Europe-America
44.9	43.5	47.2	47.6	49.0	45.6	Israel
5.9	5.9	3.9	4.2	1.6	1.4	Arabs
						1994
93.8	92.7	97.7	97.3	96.0	98.8	Jews
						Continent of birth
15.3	18.4	22.6	22.0	19.2	18.8	Asia-Africa
34.5	26.0	22.8	24.7	25.9	29.9	Europe-America
43.8	48.4	52.0	50.7	50.5	50.1	Israel
6.2	7.3	2.3	2.7	4.0	1.2	Arabs
						1998
85.2	88.5	92.0	93.2	95.0	98.3	Jews
						Continent of birth
10.1	14.4	17.0	17.8	15.0	9.8	Asia-Africa
28.8	27.0	25.0	26.9	27.0	28.8	Europe-America
45.7	47.0	51.0	48.4	53.0	59.6	Israel
14.8	11.6	8.1	6.8	4.6	1.7	Arabs

Figure 2-2. Average Annualized GDP Growth Rates, World, United States, and Israel, 1970–99

Growth rate (percent)

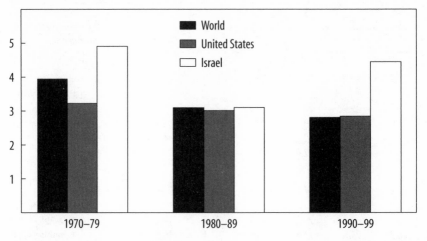

Source: International Monetary Fund, *International Financial Statistics* (various years).

economy grew at a fast enough rate to absorb so many of these immigrants—many of whom were willing to take jobs for which they were overqualified—that the national unemployment rate, which immigration helped to push from 9 to 12.5 percent in the beginning of the decade, had fallen to under 7 percent by 1996 (it then climbed to almost 9 percent, a clear result of the ambitious anti-inflation policy).

Israel can be—and is—especially proud of its high-tech sector, which has attracted foreign investment from multinational companies (largely U.S. based) and spawned numerous startup companies, many of which are now listed on U.S. stock exchanges. A negative by-product of the boom years of the 1990s, however, was the detrimental effect on income distribution. Throughout the 1990s, gaps between rich and poor widened, whereby the rich became richer and the poor (many of whom are religious Sephardim) became relatively poorer (see table 2-5). This trend concerns many in Israel, where equality in the distribution of income is a more

Table 2-5. Average Monthly Salary, by Industry, 1995 and 2000

Industry	1995	2000
Total economy (shekels)	4,355	6,771
Commerce	3,496	5,246
Public services	4,281	6,031
High-tech	7,766	14,854
Total economy (index)	100	100
Commerce	80	77
Public services	98	89
High-tech	178	219

Source: Yaakov Kop, ed., *Israel's Social Services, 2000* (Jerusalem: Center for Social Policy Research, 2000), p. 210.

important part of the national psyche than in some other countries, especially the United States.

It is important that Israelis not become too complacent with their nation's overall economic performance. The pace of economic growth, on a per capita basis, has slowed in recent years, as shown in figure 2-3. Meanwhile, persistent and rising inequality need not be the price of economic growth. The economic record of the United States provides proof. Although income inequality in the United States grew in the 1980s as the economy recovered from the 1981–82 recession, overall income growth was especially rapid during the second half of the 1990s, while income distribution remained essentially stable.[39] In the United States, the rising tide, at least recently, lifted all—or virtually all—boats.

Two of the keys to distributional success in the United States included a strong labor market—which fueled demand even for less-educated workers—coupled with a rise in the minimum wage that appeared large enough to make a difference in the income statistics but small enough not to raise the overall unemployment rate. Whether Israel can duplicate the U.S. record in the future will depend largely on the success of its macroeconomic performance, coupled with efforts to equip its less-educated workers from all religious and ethnic backgrounds with the skills necessary for higher-income jobs.

Figure 2-3. Growth of Israel's GDP per Capita, 1980–99

Thousands of shekels, 1995 prices

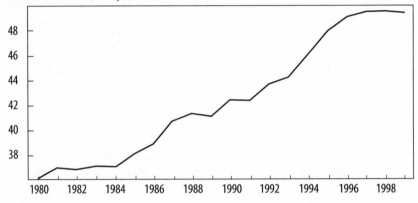

Source: Central Bureau of Statistics, *Statistical Abstract of Israel,* vol. 51 (Jerusalem: Central Bureau of Statistics, 2000), p. 6-11.

Marriage

Finally, in some societies, such as the United States, intermarriage melts away differences among ethnic, racial, and religious groups over time. For example, one analyst concluded from the 1990 census data that over half of all white Americans had spouses whose ethnic backgrounds did not overlap with their own.[40] Moreover, racial intermarriage in America has grown increasingly common.[41] So has intermarriage among Jews, which grew steadily over the postwar period and by 1990 had reached 50 percent—a level that has sparked deep concern within the Jewish community.[42]

What about exogamy—intergroup marriage—in Israel? This is especially important to Israel in light of the ethnic and religious divisions described earlier in this chapter, and because the extent of intermarriage in the future may have a powerful impact on whether and to what extent these divisions may narrow. For example, were we to find (hypothetically) that exogamy is common and likely to continue that way, then, as a broad generalization, the schisms we have identified so far probably would be of only historical significance. Demography would melt them away.

The facts are not so encouraging in this regard, however. Intermarriage cannot be counted on to narrow the Arab-Jewish divide because there are virtually no marriages between members of these groups; nor is this likely to change in the near future. The bitterness created by the Al-Aqsa uprising in both communities essentially ensures that this will be the case. The story among Jews is somewhat different. The limited data suggest that Ashkenazi and Sephardi Jews increasingly are intermarrying, which augurs well for narrowing that schism. The same trend does not appear to be true, however, for Haredim and secular Jews. Intermarriages among these two groups remain relatively rare, suggesting that the religious-secular schism within Israel is likely to remain serious for some time.

The Israeli Political System

That Israel has been a political democracy from its inception has facilitated the absorption of so many individuals from different countries and cultures. Knowing that they have a voice in their fate—through the ballot box—gives Israeli citizens, Jews and Arabs, a vital stake in making the society work. At the same time, however, certain features of Israel's parliamentary government also have facilitated fragmentation and tension.

Israel essentially borrowed its parliamentary system of government from the United Kingdom, which administered the country for several decades prior to statehood. There are advantages to such a political system, under which an entire government rests or falls on whether it continues to maintain a majority coalition of members of parliament—the Knesset in Israel.[43] As a result, in most parliamentary systems, the government speaks with one voice, and legislation and change are relatively easy to implement.

In contrast, in political systems where voting for the chief executive (a president) and the legislative branch is split, the parties controlling each branch of government can and often do differ. Such "divided" government has characterized the U.S. government for much of the postwar era. In such systems, each branch has a substantial "check" on the other, which makes it more difficult to enact legislation and effect change. At the same time, however, this flaw of republican democracies also can be a virtue. By slowing down change, such systems tend to force more compromise between the parties (and even among them) than is the case in parliamentary governments, where the majority generally does not require support from the opposition for anything it may do.

Until relatively recently, Israel's parliamentary system elected members of the Knesset, who, in turn, elected the prime minister. In 1992, the Knesset enacted electoral reform that separated voting for Knesset members and voting for the prime minister. A principal reason for the reform was to dilute the impact of the many smaller parties that existed in the country, which candidates for prime minister typically were forced to court in an effort to assemble a majority coalition. In practice, this system gave disproportionate power to a handful of small parties—typically the religious parties—whose support generally was critical to the formation of a government.

Although the ability of relatively small minority political parties to hold the balance of power in critical situations empowers members of those constituencies and gives them a stake in the political system, it has significant downsides. Small parties organized around the ethnic backgrounds or religious practices of their members reinforce the separateness of each of the groups they represent. Moreover, as the number of these parties proliferates, the political system becomes increasingly volatile. In the span of three years, 1998–2001, Israel had three different prime ministers.

In retrospect, it appears that the 1992 electoral reform—contrary to its original intent—actually contributed to political instability by *enhancing* the power of the splinter parties. As a result of the reform, Israeli voters had no need to vote for one of the larger parties (Labor or Likud, for example) in order to assure election of their desired candidate for prime minister. Instead, voters could support their favorite candidate for prime minister by voting directly for that individual and then could support one of the smaller parties in voting for the Knesset, safe in the knowledge that the Knesset vote would have no effect on the choice of prime minister (although it would affect the stability of the government). A system that encouraged splinter parties—many of which are formed around ethnic or religious groups—reinforced the divisions already present in Israeli society.

In March 2001, the Knesset voted to rescind the direct election of the prime minister and return to the previous system, a remarkable turnaround. Although the move back to the pre-1992 system is moderately encouraging, its impact should not be overstated. For reasons laid out in this chapter, Israel's political problems do not stem from the nature of its political system; rather they have much deeper roots within the society as a whole—roots that are frayed along various dimensions. In such an environment, it would be a mistake to believe that changing the nature of voting would do much to change the underlying differences among the many different factions or groups within the country. It will not.

As a result, Israel will continue to be marked by ethnic and religious politics, probably much more so than many other countries. To be sure, ethnicity, religion, and race play important roles in other democracies, including the United States. But a key difference is that, at least in the United States, the political system generally has been dominated by two parties, with third parties playing a relatively minor role—until recently, at least.[44] Of particular significance, the two political parties tend to cross ethnic—and, to a lesser extent, racial—lines. In Israel, ethnic and religious groups form their *own* political parties.

One other feature of the Israeli legal-political system also reinforces the division between secular and religious Jews. Israel is unlike most other countries in the world in *not* having a constitution. Israeli laws are enacted by the Knesset and interpreted by the Supreme Court, as in other democracies. But secular statutes are not paramount in all spheres. Because modern Israel was founded as a *Jewish* state, religious law—administered by a separate religiously based judicial system—governs sensitive areas of civil law such as marriage, divorce, and burial. As mentioned, this division of legal responsibility is a continuing source of tension between secular Israelis (many of whom resent having religious institutions govern important parts of their lives) and religious Israelis (for whom adherence to religious laws is especially important).

Moreover, these tensions have grown in recent years, as various religious parties have pressed the civil authorities to impose religious requirements—such as prohibitions on doing business on the Sabbath—on the rest of the (secular) population. The most conspicuous evidence of the backlash is the stunning success of the Shinui Party in the 1999 Knesset elections. A party that was headed for extinction at the beginning of the campaign, it won an impressive six seats in the Knesset, as we noted earlier, largely on the basis of its campaign pledge to "keep the Haredim from taking over the country." Although the large majority of secular voters supported more mainstream parties, many of them agreed with that sentiment, illustrating how deep and growing is the divide between secular and Haredi Jews.

In chapter 5, we address whether any political reforms are likely to ease the clear tensions between religious and secular Jews. Although we are not optimistic in the short run, we nonetheless believe that Israelis eventually will have to work harder at resolving the substantive differences that divide these camps if they want to preserve the pluralism to which they have become accustomed. Changes in the electoral machinery—while justified in their own right—should not be counted on to accomplish this objective.

CHAPTER THREE

Demographic
Complications

DEMOGRAPHIC FACTORS—population growth, immigration patterns, the age structure, and the like—play an important role in the development and stability of all nations. Israel is no exception. In this chapter, we explore in greater detail several demographic trends briefly mentioned in chapter 2. Beyond changes in the general population's demography, there have been particular and significant changes in the structure and size of the country's main societal groups. These demographic changes have further complicated the divisions within Israeli society.

Population Trends

Population grows because of net migration and natural means (reproduction). Given the Zionist origins of the modern state, Israeli migration has been overwhelmingly Jewish. However, in recent years Israel has taken in substantial numbers of non-Jews, mainly from the former Soviet Union, who claim to have Jewish relatives.

There also has been inward migration of Israel's Arab population, although most of the growth among Arabs is natural, due to their high birth rate: initially three times higher than Jews at the founding of the state and about twice the Jewish rate currently. One segment of the Jewish population also has a high birth rate: the Haredim, who have grown both in absolute numbers and in relative terms, due almost solely to reproduction.

The overall picture is that the two main demographic processes—migration and natural increase—have left deep imprints on the formation of Israel's large population blocs. Immigration has fueled continual growth in the Jewish sector, whereas rapid, strong natural increase in the Arab sector has offset the impact of Jewish migration. The net result is that the ratio of Jews to Arabs has remained more or less constant at 4:1 for more than four decades. The stability of this ratio is a bit misleading, however, in that both populations have experienced considerable demographic flux.

Immigration

Jewish immigration to Israel has been composed of two large waves, several smaller waves, and a small but steady inflow throughout the nation's history. Of greatest importance was the mass immigration of the early statehood period, which doubled the population within three years—a rate unmatched in Israel and anywhere else. Most of the subsequent influxes were much smaller, but the most recent wave, that of the 1990s, marked the resumption of mass immigration, as some 800,000 immigrants—most from countries that once composed the Soviet Union—arrived within a short period of time.

In total, 2.7 million immigrants arrived in Israel's first fifty years, having a decisive impact on population growth (see table 3-1). In its fifty years of existence, 42 percent of Israel's total growth has been traceable to immigration. Without immigration, the population today would be about half of what it is.

The waves of immigration have affected not only the size of the population but also its composition by groups of origin (see table 3-2). One-third of all immigrants were born in Asia and Africa, and two-thirds were born in Europe and America.[1]

Immigration at such levels obviously has had many socioeconomic effects. With a weak economy in the early years, the government had to make a tremendous effort to provide the newcomers with housing, jobs,

Table 3-1. Sources of Israel's Population Growth, 1948–98
Thousands unless otherwise noted

Population group and time period	Population at beginning of period (1)	Natural increase (2)	Migration balance Total (3)	Migration balance Immigrants (4)	Total increase (5=2+3)	Population at end of period (6=1+5)	Annual growth rate (percent) (7=5:1)	Percent of migration balance in total increase (8=3:5)
Total population								
1948–98	805.6	3,018.4	2,178.8	2,737.8	5,197.3	6,041.4	4.1	41.9
1948–60	805.6	475.4	869.4	971.1	1,344.8	2,150.4	8.2	64.6
1961–71	2,150.4	562.0	339.8	414.7	901.8	3,120.7	3.2	37.7
1972–82	3,115.6	752.7	183.5	324.9	936.0	4,063.6	2.4	19.6
1983–89	4,033.7	494.8	31.1	119.6	525.9	4,559.6	1.8	5.9
1990–95	4,559.6	465.9	593.5	702.5	1,059.4	5,619.0	3.5	56.0
1996–98	5,612.3	267.5	161.7	205.0	429.1	6,041.4	2.5	37.7
Jews								
1948–98	649.6	2,132.4	2,060.1	2,611.1	4,186.1	4,785.1	4.0	49.2
1948–60	649.6	392.3	869.3	968.7	1,261.6	1,911.2	9.2	68.9
1961–71	1,911.2	412.9	337.9	411.8	750.8	2,662.0	3.0	45.0
1972–82	2,662.0	532.5	178.6	311.9	711.0	3,373.2	2.2	25.1
1983–89	3,349.6	339.7	27.7	114.5	367.4	3,717.1	1.5	7.5
1990–95	3,717.1	291.7	540.7	659.8	832.4	4,549.5	3.4	65.0
1996–98	4,522.3	163.3	105.9	144.4	262.8	4,785.1	1.9	40.3
Non-Jews								
1948–98	156.0	886.1	118.6	126.6	1,010.8	1,256.3	4.2	11.7
1948–60	156.0	83.1	0.1	2.4	83.2	239.2	3.6	0.1
1961–71	239.2	149.1	1.9	2.9	151.0	458.7	4.5	0.3
1972–82	453.8	220.3	4.8	13.0	225.1	690.4	3.7	2.1
1983–89	684.1	155.2	3.1	5.1	158.2	842.5	3.0	2.0
1990–95	842.5	174.2	52.8	42.7	226.9	1,069.5	4.1	23.3
1996–98	1,090.0	104.2	55.9	60.5	166.3	1,256.3	4.8	33.6

Source: Central Bureau of Statistics, *Statistical Abstract of Israel*, vol. 51 (Jerusalem: Central Bureau of Statistics, 2000), p. 2-9.

consumer goods, and, in the main, staples such as food and clothing. Massive resources had to be marshaled for job creation.

Those Jews who immigrated during the first years had a harder economic time than later arrivals, but they also had the advantage of being "present at the creation." The same wave delivered most immigrants from

Table 3-2. Immigrants, by Continent of Birth

Continent of birth	Immigrants (thousands)	Percent of total immigration
Total	2,790	100
Asia	403	14
Africa	474	17
Europe	1,671	60
America	211	8

Source: Central Bureau of Statistics, *Statistical Abstract of Israel*, vol. 51 (Jerusalem: Central Bureau of Statistics, 2000), p. 5-3.

Bulgaria, Poland, and Romania. Overall, however, the immigrants from Europe and America and those from Asia and Africa were about evenly split. The early immigrants also shared their initiation to Israel, although many of those from Europe had the unique experience of being interned in immigrants' camps in Cyprus and transit camps in Europe before arriving in the country.

Although Europe was one of the two most important sources of the mass immigration immediately following the proclamation of statehood and for a number of years thereafter, the numbers have steadily dwindled over time. America was a relatively small source country of immigrants— about 1,000 to 2,000 immigrants a year in all years of statehood—but this figure rose to 10,000 in 1969 after the successful 1967 war, a one-year total that was equal to all immigration from America in the 1950s.

The second big immigration wave into Israel occurred in the 1990s, when the Soviet Union opened its gates for Jews and those who claimed to be Jews, all wanting to leave either for Israel or for the United States. As it turned out, many of the Soviets landed in Israel, beginning at the high annual pace of 200,000 and then falling to about 50,000 during the past several years. If the Soviet immigrants are counted as European (although some are from Asian areas of the former Soviet Union), then the share of European immigrants into the country rose substantially in the 1990s. Soviet immigrants also tended to be older, to have smaller families (many were single parents or individuals), and to be more highly educated than other immigrants.[2]

In the second half of the 1980s, Israel also began to take in foreign guest workers (or *gastarbeiter*). The timing can be explained by the security considerations that led the Israeli government to prevent Palestinian laborers from entering the country after various cycles of violence. For Israel, therefore, guest workers acted as a substitute for Palestinians, the traditional pool of unskilled labor for the less prestigious and lower-income jobs in Israel. Only a portion of the guest workers received formal permission to enter with this status. Many arrived under the pretense of visiting as tourists, but with the intention of staying to work. Although Israeli statistical authorities do not systematically count the number of guest workers, it is evident from casual observation that most are single males, whose labor income from Israeli sources is used primarily to support families in their home countries.

In sum, Israeli immigration has had two peaks, one early in the country's history, the other more recently, with two substantial waves in between—during the second and third decades. We next turn to natural demographic factors, which worked in opposite directions: steadily declining fertility rates had the effect of lowering population growth, while plummeting mortality rates had the effect of increasing it. Among the Jewish population, the ethnic split between the two main blocs—Asian-African (Sephardi) and European-American (Ashkenazi)—remained in rough equilibrium in most years, so this particular source of division in the country is still relevant. Nonetheless, Israel's ethnic composition has changed in different decades. After an initial period of balance between the two groups, Sephardi immigration then dominated over the first two decades. With the Soviet immigration, the pendulum has swung back.

Natural Population Increase

While immigration of Jews added to their population of the country, higher birth rates among Arabs than among Jews more than offset this effect. The net result has been a small increase in the Arab share of the Israeli population: from 18 percent in 1948 to roughly 21 percent today. Still, the reproductive record of the Jewish population in absolute numbers was impressive, considering the small size of Israel's overall population. From 1960 to 1965, for example, annual births climbed from 45,000

Figure 3-1. Total Fertility Rate among Israeli Jews and Arabs, 1955–98

Fertility rate

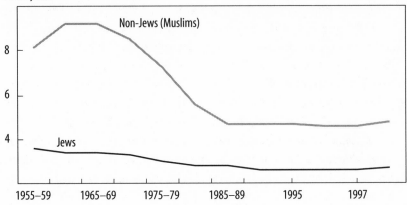

Source: Central Bureau of Statistics, *Statistical Abstract of Israel* (Jerusalem: Central Bureau of Statistics, various years).

to roughly 50,000. The absolute annual number of births kept climbing in successive five-year periods, reaching 75,000 by the mid-1970s and 90,000 by the end of 1990s.[3]

Demographers measure population growth not only in absolute numbers, but also in terms of the total fertility rate: the average number of births per woman throughout her lifetime. By this indicator, Israeli population growth through natural causes has been slowing down, as shown in figure 3-1. In 1955, the total fertility rate for Jewish women, in particular, was near 4 (3.6 for the 1955–59 period). By 1998, it had fallen to 2.7.[4]

The aggregate statistics conceal considerable variation across ethnic groups, although these differences have narrowed over time. For example, in 1955 the total fertility rates of Jewish women of Israeli or European-American origin were 2.8 and 2.6, respectively, versus a much higher rate of 5.7 for women of African-Asian origin. By 1996, however, this disparity had closed significantly: to rates of 2.7 for native-born Israelis, just 2.1 for European-Americans, and 3.1 for Asian-Africans.[5] Nonetheless, the differences in birth rates among the various groups helped to reverse the effects of immigration patterns, which have been tilted consistently toward persons of European-American origin. As reflected in table 3-3, de-

Table 3-3. Percentage of the Population of Europe-America Origin, 1948–98

Population group	1948	1960	1970	1980	1990	1998
Original population plus immigrants	85	62	59	62	63	70
Total population[a]	85	55	49	50	52	56

Source: CSPS calculations, based on Central Bureau of Statistics, *Statistical Abstract of Israel* (Jerusalem: Central Bureau of Statistics, various years).
a. Includes children born to original population and immigrants.

spite the greater numbers of the Ashkenazim in the original Jewish population and the subsequent waves of immigration, the more rapid birth rates of women of Sephardi origin have kept the overall population balance between Jews from the different groups in rough equilibrium (about 50/50) throughout most of Israel's brief history.

The contrast in fertility trends between Arab and Jewish women, however, is stark. Figure 3-1 indicates that over the 1955–98 period, the total fertility rate of an Arab woman in Israel started as high as 8, rose briefly to 9, and then fell to about 4.8, a rate well above the average for an Israeli Jewish woman.[6] The drop in births among younger Arab women, in particular, has been especially noticeable. For those ages nineteen and under, the fertility rate fell from 0.7 in 1955 to 0.25 in the early 1980s.

The differences in fertility rates, both between Jews and Arabs and among Jews of different national origins, are largely attributable to differences in income. Birth rates tend to decline with family income. Historically, lower-income families were motivated to produce more children in order to provide additional sources of labor income. As social and family incomes increased, the need to generate income through child labor declined. In addition, rising educational levels among both Arab and Jewish families have contributed to declining birth rates.[7]

The Arab population data deserve closer examination. Although official demographic statistics account for almost all of the population increase among Arabs as due to natural increase, these data ignore the fact that, over the years, some 70,000 Arab refugees have been allowed to return to Israel, many in the early years of statehood.[8] In addition, as a result of Israel's annexation of East Jerusalem, some 200,000 Arabs who

Table 3-4. Life Expectancy, by Sex and Population Group, 1949–98

| | Arabs and others | | Jews | | Total population | |
Year	Women	Men	Women	Men	Women	Men
1949	n.a.	n.a.	67.6	64.9	n.a.	n.a.
1950–54	n.a.	n.a.	70.1	67.2	n.a.	n.a.
1960–64	n.a.	n.a.	73.1	70.6	n.a.	n.a.
1970–74	71.9	68.5	73.8	70.6	73.4	70.1
1980–84	74.0	70.8	76.5	73.1	76.1	72.7
1990–94	76.3	73.5	79.2	75.5	78.8	75.1
1994–98	77.4	74.2	80.2	76.3	79.8	75.8

Source: Central Bureau of Statistics, *Statistical Abstract of Israel*, vol. 51 (Jerusalem: Central Bureau of Statistics, 2000), p. 3-30.
n.a. Not available.

previously were not counted as living in Israel now are classified as Israeli.[9] As a result, roughly 300,000 out of the 1 million increase in the Arab population attributed to natural causes is due to other factors.

Life Expectancy and Age Structure

So far, our discussion of the natural causes of population increase has been limited to births. The *net* natural increase in population, however, also is affected by the mortality rate and life expectancy. Even if the birth rate slows down, a falling mortality rate and increasing life expectancy could keep population growth relatively high. This is precisely what has happened in Israel over time.

Table 3-4 depicts patterns of life expectancy of Israeli women and men, Arabs and Jews, from 1949 through 1998. The table shows that life expectancy generally increased dramatically in the early years of the state. No further progress occurred in the 1970s, but then life expectancy continued its upward climb in the 1980s among all the groups shown. Throughout the period, however, Jews could expect to live slightly longer than Arabs.

Israel has the pleasant combination of both a lengthening life expectancy and a younger society than many other Western countries. As shown in table 3-5, the elderly account for 10 percent of the population, well below the proportions in European countries and below that in the United

Table 3-5. Age Distribution, Israel and Selected Countries, 1998

Percent

Country	0–15	15–64	65+
Australia	20.9	66.9	12.2
United States	22.2	65.9	11.9
Belgium	17.9	66.0	16.1
United Kingdom	19.2	65.1	15.7
Germany	15.5	67.9	16.6
France	19.0	65.3	15.7
Switzerland	17.6	67.3	15.1
EU-15	17.3	67.0	15.7
Israel			
Total	28.9	61.2	9.9
Jews	26.3	62.1	11.6
Arabs	42.6	54.8	2.6

Source: Organization for Economic Cooperation and Development, *OECD in Figures: Statistics on Member Countries 2000* (Paris: Organization for Economic Cooperation and Development, 2000), pp. 6–7; Central Bureau of Statistics, *Statistical Abstract of Israel*, vol. 50 (Jerusalem: Central Bureau of Statistics, 1999), p. 2-40.

States as well. At the other end of the age spectrum, Israel has a far higher percentage of children (ages birth to fourteen) than the other countries. Yet as young as Israel is today, it has aged over time. When the state was founded, for example, individuals over the age of sixty-five accounted for only 4 percent of the population.[10]

Figure 3-2 illustrates a marked disparity in the age composition of Israeli Jews and Arabs, however. A significantly greater share of the Arab population is below school age (below the age of four) than is the case for Jews. At the other extreme, a smaller fraction of Arabs are elderly, less than 3 percent, well below the 10 percent share for Israelis as a whole.[11] Within the Jewish population, a certain group—the Haredim—exhibits an age structure that looks more like that of the Arab sector than that of other Israeli Jews.

As for the rest of the Jewish population in Israel, however, the age structure looks very different: substantial numbers of young people, with most of the rest being working-age adults. In contrast, the Arab population by age looks very much like a pyramid, with the predominant share

Figure 3-2. Age Composition of Israeli Jews and Arabs, 1998

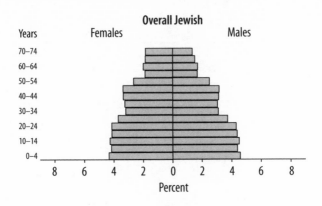

Overall Jewish

Years   Females   Males

70–74
60–64
50–54
40–44
30–34
20–24
10–14
0–4

8   6   4   2   0   2   4   6   8
Percent

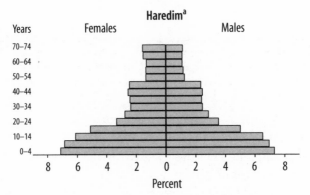

Haredim[a]

Years   Females   Males

70–74
60–64
50–54
40–44
30–34
20–24
10–14
0–4

8   6   4   2   0   2   4   6   8
Percent

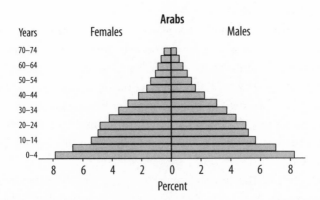

Arabs

Years   Females   Males

70–74
60–64
50–54
40–44
30–34
20–24
10–14
0–4

8   6   4   2   0   2   4   6   8
Percent

Source: Central Bureau of Statistics, *Statistical Abstract of Israel,* vol. 51 (Jerusalem: Central Bureau of Statistics, 2000), pp. 2-48–2-53.
a. As reported by one Haredi town, Bnei Barak.

among the young and steadily lower shares in the older age groups. This pyramid has been changing, however, with more and more of the Arab sector consisting of working-age adults. For example, according to Israeli census data, in 1970, those under fifteen years of age outnumbered working-age adults by 3 to 1; today, that ratio is roughly 2 to 1.

The different age structures of the Arab and Jewish populations within Israel, which are likely to persist for some time, have important socioeconomic implications. Among Arabs, for example, the relatively fewer numbers of adults must financially support a relatively larger group of dependents. This demographic burden is compounded by the fact that the average income of Arab families already is lower than that of Jewish families. The net effect is substantially lower per capita income among Arabs than among Jews, which no doubt contributes to social and political tensions.

Another important implication of the age structure relates to the demands on government resources for education. Clearly, the large numbers of young Israelis, coupled with relatively high (although declining) birth rates, mean that the educational system—for both Arabs and Jews—will have to continue to expand, taking up an ever-larger fraction of the nation's gross domestic product.

Households and Their Composition

Family household structure is also important in shaping society. In this respect, there are key differences in demographic trends between Israeli Arabs and Jews and among subgroups of these two populations. These differences have an impact on the tensions between the various groups.

In 1996, Israel had 1.5 million households and an average household size of 3.5. The average household size is larger than that of the West and reflects Israel's relatively high birth rate. But the average also conceals wide variations among groups. For example, the average is just 2.2 among "veteran" Israelis of European-American origin, 3.8 among those of African origin, and 5.5 among Arabs.[12]

The variations in household size are evident along another dimension as well. In large part because highly religious Israeli Jews tend to have large families, 15 percent of Israeli households have six persons or more.

This fraction is down somewhat from earlier periods. Nonetheless, because large households tend to be concentrated among those with lower incomes, Israeli social policy targets financial assistance through child allowances rather than income tests. Such aid today is concentrated in certain parts of the Arab sector, Haredi households, immigrants from Ethiopia, and inhabitants of various peripheral areas. Among Jews, Sephardim traditionally have benefited disproportionately from this policy because their families tend to be large and to have relatively lower incomes. Over time, as Sephardi fertility patterns have fallen in line with those of the general Jewish population, two very different groups have begun to benefit from child transfer allowances: Israeli Arabs and Haredi Jews. Until the 1990s, Arabs did not benefit fully from the allowance, since part of it was given only to those families whose household head had served in the military. This distinction was removed, and Israeli Arabs and Haredi Jews now are on equal footing in this respect.

At the opposite end of the age spectrum, ethnic differences exist in social services designed to benefit the elderly. In the past, large families tended to take care of themselves, especially as older citizens aged. Few relied on institutional help. As family size has contracted over time, institutions for the elderly funded by the state—but usually operated by non-governmental organizations—have become more important for caring for elderly residents, following a pattern in the West. Still, family-based care for the elderly tends to be prevalent among Arabs and Sephardi Jews, much more so than among Ashkenazim.

The growing economy and, along with it, rising incomes have had another important impact on household formation. Both Israeli Jews and Arabs are waiting longer to marry. Although the average age of marriage is higher among Jews than non-Jews, the gap is narrowing. For example, in the early 1960s, Jewish grooms averaged 26.4 years of age at marriage and Jewish brides averaged 22.0, whereas Arabs were roughly two or three years younger at marriage (23.5 and 19.7 years for men and women, respectively). By 1998, the age at marriage had hardly changed among Jewish men but had risen substantially among Arab men, so that the age disparity had fallen to less than two years.[13] In this respect, Israeli Jews and Arabs were becoming more alike, although many probably were unaware of that fact. Among women, a somewhat different pattern emerged.

The age at marriage rose in both population groups, but the difference between Jewish and Arab women widened.

The age at which Israeli women first have children also has been rising, as one would expect in a society with a rising standard of living. In 1960, 21 percent of first births among Jewish women were to mothers under the age of twenty. Today, very few Jewish women give birth this early. More and more they are delaying motherhood well into their twenties, and indeed 15 percent of Jewish women now have their first child after turning thirty, compared to just 5 percent in the 1960s. The pattern is very different among Arab women. Although they, too, have been delaying motherhood, a much higher fraction of Arab women have their first child under the age of twenty: 40 percent in the 1960s compared with about 25 percent today. At the other end of the age spectrum, just 5 percent of Arab women currently delay motherhood past the age of thirty.[14]

There are greater similarities between Arabs and Jews in measures of family stability. For example, although divorce generally is less frequent in Israel than in other societies—perhaps because of the significant influence of religion in sizable segments of both populations—this rate has been rising over time. Among Jews, the divorce rate doubled from 0.5 percent in 1961 to 1 percent in 1998. The divorce rate among Arabs consistently has been lower, but it more than doubled during that period, from 0.3 percent of married couples to 0.7 percent.[15]

Another indicator of family stability is the fraction of families of children with two parents. In Israel, this describes a majority of families, significantly more than in various European and North American countries. Just 11.5 percent of Israeli families are single-parent households, with no difference in this respect between Jews and Arabs.[16]

What about rates of intermarriage among Arabs and Jews? We briefly discussed this issue in chapter 2. It is a vital question for both peoples, since both place strong cultural and religious emphasis on marriage within their religion and discourage marriage outside their religion and even to some extent outside their national or ethnic group. All for good reason: the continued cohesiveness of the group or religion hinges on persuading successive generations to avoid intermarriage.

Here we offer more details on the subject. It is not a surprise that there is almost no intermarriage between Arabs and Jews. Indeed, such unions

Table 3-6.   Exogamy Patterns within the Israeli Population, 1970–98
Percent unless otherwise indicated

Indicator	1970	1980–84	1990–94	1998
Total number	23,983	24,420	25,135	30,765
Groom of Israel origin with				
Bride of Israel origin	17	24	38	44
Bride of Asia-Africa origin	28	34	31	30
Bride of Europe-America origin	55	42	31	26
Groom of Asia-Africa origin with				
Bride of Israel origin	3	6	13	22
Bride of Asia-Africa origin	78	79	70	61
Bride of Europe-America origin	18	15	17	17
Groom of Europe-America origin with				
Bride of Israel origin	6	12	19	24
Bride of Asia-Africa origin	15	26	25	22
Bride of Europe-America origin	79	63	56	55

Source: Central Bureau of Statistics, *Statistical Abstract of Israel* (Jerusalem: Central Bureau of Statistics, various years).

are so rare that Israel's Central Bureau of Statistics does not even keep track of them. At the same time, however, there is growing intermarriage between Jews of different origins, specifically those of Asian-African and European-American backgrounds (see table 3-6).[17] In fact, such marriages are becoming so common that the differences between Sephardim and Ashkenazim are growing increasingly blurred. From the vantage of those concerned about maintaining social cohesion, this is a beneficial trend.

Still, there are differences. Jews of European-American origin are more likely to marry outside their group than are Jews from Asia-Africa. For example, in 1988, the year before the great immigration from the former Soviet Union began, official statistics show that only 55 percent of Jews of European-American origin married within their group. By 1999, however, this share had increased to 70 percent.[18] In contrast, about 75 percent of Jews of Asian-African origin continued to marry within their group over the past two decades.

Unfortunately, we know much less about the rates of intermarriage between Israeli Jews of highly religious and secular backgrounds. Impressionistic evidence, however, suggests very low rates of intermarriage along this dimension. So, in this respect, divisions very much remain.

Summary of Demographic Developments

The two main sources of population growth—migration and natural increase—have left deep imprints on the formation of Israel's major groups, but in very different fashion. Whereas immigration has been the main source of population growth among Israeli Jews, natural increase has been the predominant source of growth among Arabs. The magnitudes of these two growth factors have balanced each other, so that the growth rates of the two sectors have been roughly equivalent. As a result, the 4:1 ratio of Jews to Arabs is little different than it was four decades ago.

The apparent stability of this ratio is somewhat misleading, however, because of different patterns in the sources of growth. Jewish immigration has come largely in two waves, one at the very beginning of the state and the other more recently, in the 1990s. In contrast, birth rates among Jews have been declining steadily since the founding of the state; a similar decline in births has occurred among the Arab population, but this started somewhat later, around 1960.

Among Jews, the shares of the two main ethnic blocs or groups of geographical origin—Asian-African (Sephardi) and Euro-American (Ashkenazi)—have remained in rough equilibrium in most years. But the shares have ebbed and flowed. Since most immigrants are of European-American origin, the two main waves of immigration have temporarily tilted the population balance toward this group—a shift that was rectified in the 1960–90 period by the more rapid natural increase among Jews of Sephardi origin. At the same time, a growing share of Israeli Jews have been born in Israel and are true natives. The rising share of native-born Israelis (*sabras*, as they are called) has not dulled the relatively sharp social distinctions among the different ethnic groups, but intermarriage has done so to some degree.

Age patterns within Israel also have had a significant effect on population. A rising rate of life expectancy has pushed the average age of Israelis—

both Arabs and Jews—upward. The immigration waves among Jews have had a similar effect. Nonetheless, Israel remains a relatively young society, due to a relatively high birth rate, especially within the Arab sector. Differences in age composition of Arabs and Jews almost certainly contribute to frictions between the two groups.

A Look into the Future

What about the future? As with all projections, the outcomes are very sensitive to assumptions regarding the continuation of trends in basic demographic features, such as fertility, family formation, and life expectancy. In Israel, an additional important factor is the underlying assumption about migration, both into and out of the country.[19] Bearing these cautions in mind, current official projections are still of interest, especially for the themes discussed in this book.

Israel's Central Bureau of Statistics publishes projections for the next two decades under three alternative sets of assumptions, which yield high, medium, and low scenarios. According to the most recent projection (in 2000), in the medium or "base" case, Israel's population in the year 2020 is projected to reach 8.7 million, of which 6.7 million will be Jews and 2 million will be Arabs. This increases the percentage of Arabs from 20 to 23 percent. As for age composition, 30 percent of Arabs are projected to be children ages birth to four years, while another 28 percent are projected to be youth ages fifteen to twenty-four years. (In the year 2000, children ages birth to four years old represented 16 percent of the Arab population, while youth ages fifteen to twenty-four years old represented 19 percent.)

If these projections are right, they argue even more persuasively for the need to address the current, already deep, schism between Arabs and Jews. An even younger Arab population will require even larger budget resources for education than is the case now, especially if efforts are made, as we suggest in the next chapter, to upgrade the quality of education within that segment of the population. To underscore this point, we have carried out our own population projections, extended to cover a longer period. By the year 2050, given a medium set of assumptions, Israel's total population will be over 12 million, and the Arab component will be close to

35 percent. Furthermore, the share of Arabs ages birth to fourteen years will be 46 percent, while the ratio of Arab to Jewish children will be about even (despite the continuing disparity in the number of Jews and Arabs overall)!

Clearly, these projections emphasize how much more difficult and complicated it will be in the future for Israel to maintain both a "Jewish state" and a democracy.

It is more difficult to project the relative size of various blocs within the Jewish population. Intermarriage probably will moderate the Ashkenazi-Sephardi split, and social and economic developments might lower even further the remaining tensions between these two ethnic groups. In one sector—the Haredim—the demographic trends favor continued growth. Their pattern of fertility has proven to be very effective in recent decades in increasing their share in the Jewish population, but it remains to be seen whether they will be able to afford such high birth rates, while continuing to avoid participation in the labor force.

Overall, Israeli Jews are expected to maintain their relatively young age composition for the following decades. Most Jewish groups (excluding Haredim) will become older, but by far less than the developed world. Even in 2020, those sixty-five or older are not likely to exceed 12 percent of the population, far below the fraction in other developed countries.

CHAPTER FOUR

Bridging
the Divides

ALTHOUGH ISRAEL GOES about as far as any country in the world to welcome individuals of varied backgrounds and to help them integrate into the mainstream of the nation's culture and society, these efforts, although formally universal, are not so in actuality. They do not extend to the same degree, for example, to Arab citizens, who have the same basic formal civil rights as other Israelis, but not the same economic opportunities. Furthermore, Israeli Jews are divided—in some cases, deeply so—by country of birth, ethnic group, income, and religious practice. Indeed, three groups of Israelis—the recent Russian immigrants, Haredi Jews, and Arab citizens, who collectively account for about 40 percent of the population—share almost nothing with each other in the way of cultural background and relatively little with the rest of Israel's Jewish population.

In its early years, Israel had no other choice than to try to "melt" away at least the ethnic differences between Jewish natives and newly arriving Jews. The immigrants came to Israel holding few possessions and speaking different languages. Following the searing experience of the Holocaust and the uncertainty of living day to day in refugee camps in Europe, Israel offered hope and opportunity for building a new life.

Correspondingly, hundreds of thousands of Jewish refugees abandoned their native Arab countries in the wake of the 1948 war between their countries and the Jewish state. The great majority of these immigrants arrived with an educational background that was hardly suitable for the local social and economic environment. With little physical or human capital, they faced great difficulties integrating into a social structure dominated, from the outset, by natives and European immigrants.

To make matters worse, Israel was largely a barren country and, by modern standards, very much underdeveloped. Yet sometimes necessity truly is the mother of invention. Times were tough, and immigrants and many natives shared a common fate. These conditions made it easier for the country's leaders—and especially its educators—to instill shared values and culture. In an ironic twist, it was easier in Israel's early days to implement policies designed to melt away what, at that time, were especially large social and cultural differences.

Several institutions were instrumental in this process: a common language (Hebrew), substantial economic and educational assistance for all immigrants, mandatory military service for both men and women (although the social aspect was not the main purpose of military service), a national educational system, and, as the country grew richer, a gradually expanding safety net for the aged, infirm, and economically disadvantaged. These same institutions continue, but now are pursued under a very different model—what might best be called institutional pluralism—that attempts to accommodate and ideally (but, in fact, imperfectly) tolerate the many cultural and ethnic differences of Israeli citizens.

Israel's Arab population, however, has never been subject to the melting pot process, nor has it been well embraced by the Jewish institutions that dominate the country. Arabs have lived separately, have not been integrated occupationally, and have been educated in their own subsystem. Arabs in the main do not serve in the military. This separate—and in many respects admittedly unequal—treatment has been partly due to security concerns. To put it bluntly, there were Israeli Jews who feared at the outset that Arab citizens represented a potential fifth column living in their midst and acted accordingly. It is not surprising, therefore, that Arab-Jewish relationships have been awkward at best and openly hostile at worst.

However, some Israeli officials—and perhaps much of the country—also believed that the separation of Arabs and Jews served the interests of the Arabs themselves. The Arab education system is an example. The Israeli government intended to maintain a separate system for Arab children so that they could converse in their mother tongue and study subjects relevant to their own culture and history. Nonetheless, many Arab scholars, and some Jews as well, saw in this arrangement another means of oppression and coercion.[1]

In any event, Arabs are citizens of the state and are allowed to run for office and serve in the Israeli Knesset.[2] Still, many (if not most) Arabs feel that, since Israel is defined as a "Jewish state" and not as a "state of all its citizens," they are second-class citizens and thus question how much they really belong in Israel. So, too, do many Jews. These undercurrents exist despite the fact that the Israeli government, over time, has attempted to improve its treatment of Arab citizens, explicitly encouraging their integration into Israeli society in all dimensions. It is reasonable to assume, although we cannot prove it, that had these efforts been even more intense than they have been, there would be significantly less tension between Jews and Arabs today.

A lot has happened over the years to deepen the divide between the two peoples, of which the Al-Aqsa uprising among the Palestinian population that began in the fall of 2000 is the most recent example. It is far from clear whether a sustained effort to improve relations between Arabs and Jews would succeed in muting resentments within the Arab community. There may be too much water over the dam, so to speak, to change hardened attitudes on both sides. Notwithstanding these difficulties, we offer some suggestions in chapter 5 for attempting a rapprochement, for moral as well as political reasons. A fundamental fact remains: as the discussion of demographic trends in chapter 3 makes very clear, Arab citizens will continue to be a significant part of Israeli society in the future, and their treatment is a key issue that simply cannot be ignored.

Meanwhile, Israel faces a stiff challenge in ensuring that Israeli Jews have a sufficient set of common values, beliefs, knowledge, and experiences to maintain a reasonable degree of cohesion, at least among themselves. The difficulty of that challenge tends to be obscured or ignored when security threats occupy the public's attention. Our hope is that the security problems will diminish one day. But then each of the institutions described in this chapter must function with even greater effectiveness if Israeli society, including both its Jews and its Arabs, is not to fragment even further. In any event, the improvement of these institutions should not be postponed until the security problems are resolved; both goals have to be pursued simultaneously.

A Common Language

A common language is one way for citizens to develop a common bond.[3] That bond did not exist before modern Israel became a state. Although Jews lived alongside Arabs in what was then the British Mandate of Palestine, not all Jews spoke Hebrew. It was only at the end of the nineteenth century, when Eliezer ben-Yehuda—a dedicated dreamer—launched a successful drive to revitalize Hebrew (which was used almost exclusively in biblical study and in Jewish prayers), that it was adopted and converted into a modern everyday language. Even then, many Jews continued to speak Yiddish, Ladino, and languages other than Hebrew. Moreover, not all Jewish schools taught their students in Hebrew.

This gradually changed in the first half of the twentieth century. When the modern state of Israel was founded, one of the first tasks of its new leaders was to establish Hebrew as the major official language.[4] The principal reason for doing so was to give the highly diverse population, speaking many different languages, one language in common.[5] As the state language, Hebrew was—and still is—used in all official business and in the school system. At the same time, from the early years of the state, Jewish children have been taught English as a second language. In Arab schools, however, children are taught in Arabic, although in upper grades, they also are taught Hebrew and English as secondary languages.

Israeli authorities have gone to great lengths to ensure that Jewish immigrants quickly learn to be conversant in Hebrew. On their arrival, they are enrolled in an intensive *ulpan* course designed to ensure that they can speak, read, and write the language. Furthermore, in the early years of the state immigrants were encouraged to take on new Hebrew names.[6] Symbolically,

Israelis in the diplomatic corps were even required to take Hebrew names when stationed in a foreign country.

The use of modern Hebrew in the schools and among adults in daily life has done much to foster a distinctive Israeli culture—manifested in the nation's literature, poetry, film, and theater. In a society of immigrants, the Hebrew language provides a powerful unifying force. Nonetheless, in recent years, the overall exclusiveness of the language seems to be weakening somewhat. Many immigrants continue to use their own language among themselves, as is the case in other countries. Some also object to the compulsory training in Hebrew, although, as a practical matter, immigrants sacrifice a great deal if they do not become proficient in the language of other Israelis.[7] It is harder to gain access to well-paying jobs and to become fully integrated economically and socially without the ability to write and speak Hebrew with ease. .

One exception to this broad statement is that English is the language of instruction in colleges and graduate schools, especially for scientific subjects, where most of the cutting-edge research is written in English. In addition, English is often spoken in high-tech firms where employees have day-to-day contact with Americans or others from the West, either in person or through electronic or telephonic communication.[8] Nonetheless, outside these few locales, Hebrew remains very much the dominant language, and even those relatively few students and professors who conduct their research and classes in English speak Hebrew with their friends and colleagues outside class.

Immigrant Absorption

From the outset of the state's young history, Jewish immigrants have been welcomed with open arms, granted immediate citizenship (unlike the multiyear waiting periods in Australia and the United States), and given substantial economic assistance and advice—a constellation of initial benefits that far surpasses anything made available to immigrants anywhere else in the world, to our knowledge.[9] Moreover, the Jewish Agency—a privately supported nongovernmental organization founded in the 1920s for welfare assistance to the Jews—continues to provide transportation assistance to immigrants coming to Israel. The size and content of these benefits have changed over time, becoming more generous as the country has grown richer.

The *Olim*—the Hebrew term for the new arrivals—are eased into Israeli society through various measures.[10] All immigrants are given a crash *ulpan* course in Hebrew—running five days a week, five hours a day for six months and often more—along with a cash grant and rent subsidy while they are learning Hebrew. In the early years of the country, the initial absorption and language instruction took place in the poorly furnished transit sites in which immigrants were settled temporarily. Later, the government built absorption centers to house and train the new immigrants.

Many of the immigrants originally were directed or encouraged to live in "development towns" and in rural settlements in peripheral areas—to avoid further congesting Israel's main urban areas and to inhabit outlying border areas.[11] Many of the new towns did not have viable economic development potential. Government authorities often ignored the original occupations of the immigrants (most were artisans and merchants, some were professional practitioners) and assigned them to farm or factory labor, for which they had no background, training, or desire. Furthermore, employment in the development towns tended to be centralized in a small number of plants that could not survive without continued government aid.

To its credit, over the years the Israeli government recognized these problems with the "population dispersion" strategy and began to allow the "direct absorption" of most immigrants, allowing them to choose their place of residence and employment, with government subsidies. Even this policy has had mixed success, however. Because housing is so much more expensive in central cities, the Soviet immigrants of the 1990s have clustered in peripheral areas where employment opportunities are scarce. As Russian immigrants find new jobs, they are moving away from their enclaves, but this is proving to be a gradual process.

By 1996, more than half of the new immigrants from the former Soviet Union had acquired permanent housing.[12] A large number of immigrants who were placed in development towns managed to establish themselves and to become strongly involved in their local municipalities and politics. The difficulties these immigrants face have helped to forge common bonds—indeed, so much so that Russian immigrants, in particular, have developed allegiance to their own political party, strengthening their voice in national affairs but at the price of weakening the dominant political parties, Labor and Likud.

Once they leave absorption centers, or even if they are absorbed directly, all immigrants continue to be eligible for preferential housing loans for seven years and for reduced property taxes if they purchase a residence; for reduced rent in public housing (mostly located in outlying areas and subject to multiyear waiting lists) if they are elderly or have family members with disabilities; and for various other economic benefits, including immediate eligibility for social welfare programs.[13]

The open-arms policy toward Jewish immigrants has legal status and is embodied in the Law of Return, which since 1950 has entitled to immediate citizenship any individual defined to be Jewish. Because it is inherently discriminatory, the Law of Return has long been a source of friction between Arabs and Jews. Of course, by limiting automatic immigration to Jews, Israel has made it easier, at least for these new arrivals, to melt into the prevailing culture. This is true only to a very limited extent, however. For one thing, most Jewish arrivals do not know or strictly adhere to standard Jewish rituals. This is especially true for immigrants from the former Soviet Union, whose communist regime made every effort to stamp out religious practices of all kinds. Furthermore, among Jews who may be termed "religious," there are great differences—in national origin, in local customs, and in native language—that can and often do loom larger than the common "religious" bond (which, for some, is viewed as little more than an accident of birth). Still, the national bond, in addition to some religious background, does lay a foundation of common creed and feeling that promotes the melting process.

As with any policy, the immigrant absorption process has had its bumps. For example, as we have noted, the immigration of Ethiopian Jews in the 1980s and early 1990s did not go as smoothly as the immigration of individuals of other nationalities. Among the obvious reasons were their relatively low educational attainment and lack of workplace skills. More broadly, the extraordinary combination of benefits conferred on Jewish immigrants has become a source of friction and, indeed, resentment among some native Israelis—both Jews and Arabs—who see each wave of immigrants as posing competition for limited resources, while bringing new (often unwelcome) values and burdens to Israeli society (although, in fact, economic prosperity has followed each of the two major waves of Israeli immigration). All in all, however, the extensive efforts made by successive Israeli governments to absorb immigrants into the mainstream of Israeli society clearly have facilitated the transition of immigrants to new lives, while keeping the schisms discussed in chapter 2 from widening further.

The Military

From the founding of the state, Israel has had compulsory military service. The service requirement is not just for the young or for males. While all Israeli males must serve a three-year term once they turn eighteen, they remain obligated for one month a year thereafter until they reach the age of fifty. Israeli women also must serve in the army, albeit for much shorter periods and in noncombat roles (with some rare exceptions made recently— pilots and naval officers).[14] Immigrants are given a grace period before being recruited for military service and, if justified by their age or family status, often are granted shorter periods of service.

The military service requirement not only has met the clear and vital objective of protecting the nation but also has had important collateral benefits. Just as the draft during World War II helped to fuse an entire generation of Americans from different backgrounds, the universal service obligation has done the same for successive generations of Israelis. Indeed, the military has become the central instrument for imparting Israeli values and culture, as well as the Hebrew language, to the large numbers of Jewish immigrants who have poured into the country over the years. The Israeli army also mixes individuals of varied backgrounds, who forge lifelong friendships and networks that are useful, if not essential, for gaining access to jobs and contracts throughout adult life. In fact, so strong are the ties formed in the army that individuals who do not serve, or are not allowed to serve, or are exempted from serving (as in the case of Israeli Arabs, for example) are effectively locked out of the upper reaches of Israeli business and social elites.

The Israeli military service requirement has been weakening over time, however, and with it some of the "social glue" that the armed forces provided also has been dissolving, making way for deeper divisions over military service. Today, less than 60 percent of Israeli men are drafted into the Israeli army,[15] only a third serve active reserve duty, and only a fraction serve in reserve combat units. As more citizens are exempted from service, those who serve bear a growing resentment toward those who do not. This is not a healthy social—or, arguably, military—development. Much of the resentment has been directed at the Haredi sector. In 2000, the government created the Tal Commission to explore options for creating some form of service for Haredi youth. However, the Haredi leadership vetoed the commission's recommendations.

Education

One of Israel's greatest successes has been the vast improvement in its educational institutions and the training of its people. In the early years of statehood, not only was the general educational level of the population, mainly the immigrants, relatively low, but there were also great disparities between Arabs and Jews and among Jewish subgroups. From these humble beginnings, Israel has built an impressive educational system. Its K–12 schools generally provide high-quality training. Several of the country's universities are among the world's best, and graduate students are as well trained, especially in the fields of science and technology, as those from leading universities in the West.

The Israeli educational system has reflected the same shift away from the ethos of the melting pot and toward pluralism that has marked the rest of society and also is present in other countries, notably the United States.[16] To some extent, this shift has been healthy, encouraging more choice and diversity. But there are some worrying aspects, raising questions of equity in educational funding and perhaps ultimately of how to maintain the cohesive function that education provides to new generations (along with the skills needed to function in an increasingly technological society).

When the state was founded, the Israeli educational system was very much an instrument of the melting pot ideology, at least for the Jewish population. The schools gave little or no attention to different Jewish cultures or practices. Various secular subjects, such as music, history, and geography, were taught through a European-Israeli lens. Moreover, Israeli Jews learned relatively little about Jewish life outside Israel (the Diaspora).

Table 4-1. Pupils in Israeli Primary Schools, 1970–2000

Indicator and type of education system	1970	1980	1990	2000
Number of pupils (thousands)				
Primary education	461	546	601	747
Hebrew	376	424	462	564
State	246	315	328	343
Private religious	129	109	133	221
Arab	85	122	139	183
Grade 1				
Hebrew	48	65	70	85
State	33	50	50	52
Religious	16	16	20	33
Arab	11	19	21	29
Hebrew share (percent)				
Primary education				
State	66	74	71	61
Private religious	34	26	29	39
Grade 1				
State	68	76	72	61
Private religious	32	24	29	39

Source: Central Bureau of Statistics, *Statistical Abstract of Israel* (Jerusalem: Central Bureau of Statistics, various years).

Over time, however, the nation's school system has become more fragmented and, in the process, has become less concentrated on imparting common values and beliefs to the country's children. In contrast to the early decades of the state, when Israeli elites favored uniformity in education, Israeli parents have increasingly demanded the right to choose their children's schools, primarily for educational reasons (another parallel to the United States). The fragmentation of the educational system is especially evidenced by the growing fractions of students from highly religious families, whose children attend either state-run or independent Haredi schools (see table 4-1). Typically, the fostering of symbols, identities, and styles by the constituents of the education system (state, state-religious, and independent) stresses each constituent's own elements alongside the symbols, identities, and consciousness that all pupils may share.[17] This phenomenon reflects Israeli social processes, and these policies have allowed the system to develop without bridging the divide. Perhaps the leaders of the Israeli education system who allowed matters to advance in this direction failed to realize that the system had begun to foster separatist styles and ways of life.

The nascent "choice" movement in the secular state school system seems to be contributing to separatism as well. This need not be the result of more parental choice. But in practice more choice—and diversity among schools—is being pursued by ensuring that school populations are socially homogenized, through the creation of magnet schools, charter schools, open enrollment, experimental schools, and special-skills schools (all options found in the United States). As a result, the enrollment patterns at some state schools not only reflect existing social stratifications but also may even contribute to their perpetuation. Although so far only a small percentage of the country's parents have taken advantage of the new educational options, if dissatisfaction with the performance of the secular school system grows (as it has in the United States), more choice unintentionally could encourage more separatism.

The state-religious system also has begun to exhibit several splintering trends: the tendency to separate boys from girls (either by establishing separate schools or by establishing separate classes in the same schools); segregationist policies on the part of principals (to the extent of preventing encounters with schools of other sectors); and the fostering of elitist education (as in *yeshiva* high schools and the girls' equivalent, the *ulpena*), typified by high educational standards, compulsory commitment to a strictly religious way of life, and the characteristic political activism that is spread among major parts of the nation's religious public.[18] However, unlike the splintering forces in the secular system, which put individuals and their self-fulfillment at the forefront, the result (and the objective) in the state-religious schools is to foster social cohesion among the student populations at those institutions.

The Arab educational system also has its own separatist features. Indeed, since independence was proclaimed, not only have members of the Arab minority been allowed to attend separate schools in their localities and in mixed towns such as Acre, Haifa, and Jaffa, but the Israeli government actually has supported a totally separate educational system for Arab children.[19] Instruction in Arab schools continues to be conducted in Arabic, although Arab children learn Hebrew as a secondary language (in addition to English, which is the most common second language in Jewish schools). Not only is this situation unlikely to change, but leaders within the Arab sector have begun to call for even greater autonomy and more separation from the general Jewish educational system. Arab parents take great pride in both their language and their heritage, a pride reinforced by the increasingly volatile political situation. Moreover, the segregated Arab school system lets the Arab public disengage from the schools attended by Israeli Jews that promote symbols alien and, in part, unacceptable to Arabs.

The separate Arab educational system thus acts as both a manifestation of pluralism and a constraint on how well Arabs can be integrated into the Israeli economy and political system. Israeli Jews have mixed views about this result. While some Israelis worry that the development of a separate set of Arab symbols and identities exacerbates existing tensions and divisions between Jews and Arabs, the majority of Israeli Jews accept the separatist approach to Arab education largely because they do not want Arab children to mix with Jewish children.

Just as the school system has evolved in a pluralistic direction, so too have the nation's matriculation examinations, which are required in Israel both to receive a high school diploma and to enroll in a university. Originally established as a set of uniform tests that all Israeli children (Arab and Jewish) were required to take if they wanted to continue their formal education after high school, the tests have become more flexible. Now students have more choice in the selection of the subjects and levels for examination. Even the curricula of the schools, as well as the textbooks, have changed, promoting a more multicultural approach that even gives some place in Jewish schools to Arab and Palestinian literature and achievements.[20] All this has occurred while more Israelis have been qualifying for their matriculation certificates, as shown in figure 4-1.

Although diversity in schools is not limited to Israel—the United States, for example, has long vested localities with control over their own schools—in Israel's case, an increasing number of children from different ethnic and religious backgrounds are being educated in schools with different curricula and educational philosophies. In the United States, children of richer

Figure 4-1. Percentage of Seventeen-Year-Olds Eligible for Matriculation Certificates, 1965–99

Percent

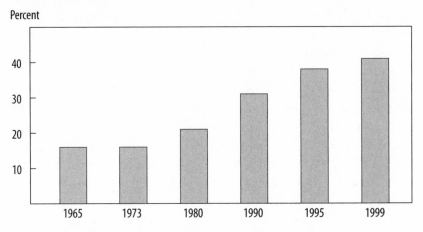

Source: Ministry of Education, *Facts and Figures, 2001* (Jerusalem: Ministry of Education, 2001), p. 72.

families attend schools that benefit from more nongovernmental resources than is the case for children from poorer families, and this trend is beginning to occur in Israel as well. For example, many Israeli schools now collect voluntary parent fees to supplement the formal Israeli education with additional instruction.[21] Another source of division is that Haredi schools teach little or nothing about the virtues of growing up and living in a political democracy or about science and English (tools required in the world of work).

Overall, as shown in figure 4-2, Israel poured increasing resources into K–12 schooling per pupil during the early 1990s (with the figure leveling off after 1996). At the same time, Israel's central government has tried to offset some of the disparities in educational funding among school districts since the 1960s, when they were first recognized as a problem, by steering proportionately more money to schools serving lower-income areas. But the resources have not matched the needs. Currently, only a fraction of the Education Ministry's budget has been earmarked directly for lower-income areas, too small a sum to achieve a major narrowing of the gap in educational attainment between children of Israel's two major ethnic

Figure 4-2. Government Spending per Pupil on Education, 1990–2000

Current budget, thousands of shekels, constant prices

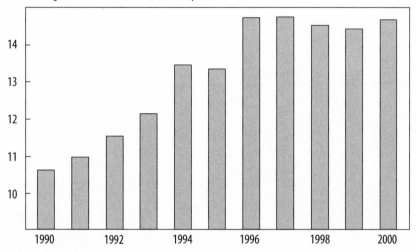

Source: Center for Social Policy Studies in Israel.

groups (Ashkenazim and Sephardim). Nonetheless, the educational system has succeeded in one significant respect: the share of teenagers who neither attend school nor hold a job has been declining steadily over the past two decades (see figure 4-3).

There are also funding disparities between different types of schools. Among the schools for Israeli Jews, those in the state-religious system receive more money per class and per pupil than secular schools. On the surface, this difference in funding may appear to be the product of the political clout of the religious parties. But a deeper look into the data reveals a more complicated situation. Religious schools receive more money, in part, because the families of their students tend to have lower incomes than the families of children in secular schools. In the same vein, parents' right to choose between secular and religious state education for their children is protected by law. As a result, some religious schools are open even when the number of students is very small. The classes in these religious schools have fewer pupils than their secular state counterparts, in part because of the requirement that boys and girls learn separately. Since

Figure 4-3. Percentage of Israeli Youth Ages Fifteen to Seventeen Who Neither Attend School nor Work, 1980–99

Percent

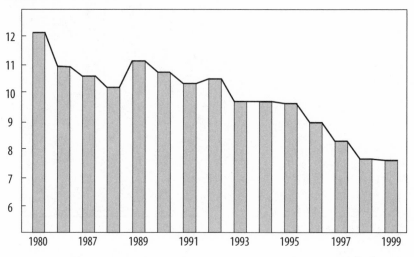

Source: Central Bureau of Statistics, *Statistical Abstract of Israel* (Jerusalem: Central Bureau of Statistics, various years).

budgetary resources are allotted by class, and not by pupil, the religious schools are effectively subsidized relative to the secular state schools—a situation that accentuates, rather than reduces, differences.

There are also significant resource disparties between the relatively less-well-funded state-supported Arab schools and Jewish schools. As a result, throughout Israel's history, classes in Arab schools have been larger, and classrooms and auxiliary facilities have been less well equipped than their Jewish counterparts. Furthermore, as of the mid-1990s, Arab schools devoted approximately five hours less per week to instruction.[22]

Given the resource disparities in the primary and secondary schools, it is not surprising that marked disparities in university enrollment continue to exist among children of different groups. The largest discrepancies, as one might expect, are between Arabs and Jews. In 1999, 46 percent of Jews qualified for higher education, 50 percent more than the 31 percent of Arabs who also did so. Nonetheless, there has been significant progress among the Arab student population. In 1960, just 2 percent of Arab students passed the matriculation exam, compared with 11 percent of Jews.[23] The disparities in college eligibility are not as great among different groups of Jewish students, although they exist. For example, as of 1999, 52 percent of children of Ashkenazi origin qualified for college attendance by passing the national matriculation examination, compared with 38 percent of children of Sephardi families, although the latter were increasing their eligibility at a more rapid pace than the former. The matriculation rates of Jewish students in the state general track are not significantly different from the rates in the state-religious schools, however.[24]

In sum, a tension continues between the aspiration of the Israeli authorities to enhance cohesion among Israel's future citizens and the desire to respond to the ethnic, religious, and nationalistic preferences of society's various constituencies. This tension is gradually being resolved in favor of diversity, which, although it satisfies the public's desire for choice, is moving Israeli society steadily away from its original melting pot ideal.

Social Services

Although not immediately apparent as an instrument of social blending, Israel's gradually expanding safety net for especially needy individuals also has provided some of the glue that has held the country together through the years (although it has not necessarily been part of an explicit melting pot policy). The current safety net includes a social security program that provides retirement income, survivor's benefits, and child support;[25] unemployment insurance; training programs for unemployed workers; and a national health insurance program. Table 4-2 illustrates that Israel has devoted an increasing share of its total output to social spending (which includes all of the above programs plus education, which is the largest category of social expenditures) as its defense needs have diminished. Immigrants are provided a broader, but temporary, safety net than native Israelis in order to ease them into Israeli society.

Meanwhile, Israel's continued economic growth has helped the country to finance improvements in health care, diet, and social services that have led to longer life expectancies for Arabs and Jews, men and women. Chapter 3 shows these improvements, although small disparities between Arabs

Table 4-2. Israeli Government Spending as a Percentage of Gross Domestic Product, 1980–2000

Year	Total	Social programs	Defense	Other
1980	57	15	22	12
1990	46	16	13	9
2000	41	20	9	7

Source: Yaakov Kop, ed., *Israel's Social Services 1999–2000* (Jerusalem: Center for Social Policy Studies, 2000), p. 26.

and Jews remain (disparities by gender are a well-known phenomenon everywhere).

Social services are funded and administered primarily by the national government.[26] However, municipal governments deliver such traditionally local services as the maintenance of schools, personal welfare and other services, and refuse removal. As in other countries, differences in the resources available to municipal governments—reflecting differences in the incomes of their residents—translate into differences in the level of social services across the country. The richer, older communities tend to offer more or different services than are available in newer communities or in those with large concentrations of families of lesser means.

To some extent, religious and political organizations within Israel help to balance out the inequities by funding and delivering services to their constituencies. Financial assistance from Jews in the Diaspora also helps to level the playing field. In recent years, nongovernmental foreign aid has represented about 10 percent of total inflows of foreign capital by the public sector (or 5 percent of total unilateral transfers). To be sure, some of this aid goes to institutions and activities that are not engaged in aiding the disadvantaged, such as Israeli universities and hospitals. But much is channeled directly into supporting social services within Israel.

In theory, some portion of the private monies supporting social services displaces government funding that otherwise would be provided, so not all of the assistance adds to total spending. But there are limits to how much more deeply involved Israeli governments would be in the absence of such private support. Taxes in Israel are very high compared to taxes in the United States, as shown in figure 4-4, in part because of heavy de-

Figure 4-4. Tax Burden in Israel and the United States, 1970–98

Percent of GDP

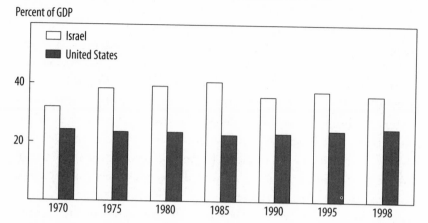

Source: Office of Management and Budget, *Annual Report, 2000,* vol. 50 (Jerusalem: Treasury Ministry, 2001), p. 248.

mands for spending on national defense. Military expenditures still account for 10 percent of Israel's gross domestic product, more than double that of the United States and one of the highest proportions in the world.

The Media and Entertainment

Not to be overlooked is the powerful influence of the media and entertainment in any society, and Israel is no exception. Here, too, history has moved in one direction: from a relatively homogeneous media that reinforced common bonds among Israelis to a media and entertainment culture that is highly diverse, catering to various ethnic and religious groups, much as has occurred in the United States and other countries over the past several decades.[27]

Homogeneity was enforced in the early years of the state because most newspapers were publicly owned and operated by the political parties, while the only electronic medium—radio—was totally controlled and operated by the government. Once television came to Israel, the government, through the Israel Broadcast Authority, owned that, too.

By the late 1960s, a backlash developed against state-dominated media. Critics complained about the politicization of public broadcasting. Sephardim argued that the state radio and television ignored them, providing little programming or entertainment aimed at the Sephardi population. Eventually, the government loosened its control, privatizing and liberalizing media ownership. A second government television channel, operated by a consortium of private companies, and cable television were introduced, bringing in many channels from around the world. Local radio stations were established, and local, sectarian, ethnic, and religious newspapers proliferated. The media began to develop the same degree of diversity as the Israeli population, with different channels, newspapers, and magazines targeting various constituencies in different languages: Hebrew, Arabic, and Russian. The media, in Israel and in other countries where there is a lot of choice, now contribute to the fragmentation of society. Specialized media appeal to various ethnic and religious groups, reinforcing the differences among them.

There is another crosscurrent within the media industry, however: a high degree of ownership concentration, as is also true in industrial countries (and throughout the developing world). Within Israel, a handful of families—Mozes, Schocken, Nimrodi, and Fishman—control very large segments of the electronic and print media. It is not clear which of these competing forces—growing diversity and a high degree of ownership concentration—will "win out" or whether they will coexist side by side, as has occurred in the United States.

The same forces of homogeneity and diversity are found in Israeli music, which is of three broad genres—"Eretz Israel" (Israeli folk music), Israeli pop/rock (which is heavily influenced by Western music), and Mediterranean/Mizrachi music (appealing primarily to Sephardim)—as well as many smaller genres (religious, Arab, and Russian). This broad diversity of music types, appealing to different segments of the population, is markedly different from the more homogeneous Eretz Israel songs that were dominant during the initial years of the state.

The growing diversity of Israeli music has not emerged without struggle. The currently popular Mediterranean music, which heavily reflects Middle Eastern and Arabic influences, initially was perceived as "foreign" and resisted by Israeli record companies. The creators and artists of this new music nonetheless found a way to distribute it through cassettes, accounting for its nickname, "Cassette Music." By the 1990s, Mizrachi music had gained a firm foothold as one of the three main forms of Israeli popular music, together with Israeli pop/rock and folk. All three struggle against Western, especially American, pop/rock to maintain their time in the limelight.[28]

Disillusionment with Pluralism in the 1990s

The 1990s in Israel witnessed the dramatic events of renewed mass immigration, economic boom, and the peace process. But this decade had its share of disillusionments that sharpened some of the major divides in Israeli society and threatened the pluralistic nature of the country. Certain myths and core assumptions were challenged; income inequalities persisted and, depending on how they are measured, grew; shifts occurred along the political spectrum; and Israelis raised questions about the meaning and implications of "Jewish and democratic" as their definition for the nature of their state. It is not surprising that these disillusionments were accompanied by a resumption of social and political tension, the extreme manifestation being the assassination of Prime Minister Yitzhak Rabin.

The national mood has swung very strongly during and after some of the major events of the decade. Geopolitical and military developments of the Gulf War and its aftermath ended the first Intifada (which had started in December 1987), and this chain of events led to the peace summit in Madrid, attended by Israel and its neighboring Arab countries under wide international auspices. Concurrently, Israel rather smoothly absorbed hundreds of thousands of former Soviet immigrants, although the process was painful for many. The switch of government from Likud to Labor enabled the Oslo accords, at the cost of increasing the internal political divide. At the same time, socioeconomic gaps continued to widen, as not all population groups shared the fruits of the new atmosphere of peace.

The ups and downs of the peace process ultimately led to the greatest disillusionment of the decade. It did not seem to start out that way. The decade began with a sense of euphoria, at least among the majority of Israelis, following an interim agreement with the Palestinians. But a large minority of the population disapproved or at least were extremely wary of the "peace process" and thus had to live with a new reality, which negated the vision of a Greater Israel—the idea of expanding Israel's borders to include all of the biblical Land of Israel through settlement activity. As the peace process gathered momentum, many former adherents abandoned this view, seemingly paving the way for an ultimate peaceful resolution of the Palestinian question. The government's withdrawal from Hebron, carried out by the Likud government under Benjamin Netanyahu, was perhaps the most dramatic illustration of this shift in opinion because the city was controlled by the main proponents of a Greater Israel.

At the same time, the goal of many in the "peace camp"—the "New Middle East" championed by Shimon Peres based on the model of the European Union, with better relations built through the opening of borders and economic cooperation—proved to be unrealistic. This became evident even before the breakdown of the peace process and the latest and most violent Intifada launched in late September of 2000. The advocates of the peace process have since been weakened significantly; many have switched sides altogether and now take a much harder position on dealing with the Palestinian question.

Meanwhile, for those in the broad center of Israel's political system, the internal struggle over the cultural character of the state proved to be a surprising disappointment as well. Israel's social and cultural life used to be predominantly secular. The nation's main social and cultural affairs were handled from the very beginning of the modern state from a secular perspective, although with an openness toward the aspirations of the religious population and basic Jewish tradition. In the 1980s, however, the tide began to shift, as the growing fraction of the population that can be characterized as highly religious began to assert itself more strongly in political and social affairs. The best symbol of the new mood was the rise of a new Haredi party, Shas. At the same time, however, a counterbalancing force also emerged: the large wave of immigrants from the former Soviet Union in the 1990s, who were seen by the secular public—largely Ashkenazi—as a potential ally in their commitment to keep the state and its affairs as secular as they were at the outset. This did not come to pass. While the new immigrants were indeed secular, the growing political power of the religious parties, and the Haredim in particular, outweighed any secularizing impact of the Soviet immigration, while the gulf in outlook and values of the religious and secular "camps" continued to widen.

More broadly, a major shift occurred over the past quarter century in the power structure of the country. In its early decades, Israel was marked by a struggle of peripheral groups against the political center—the elite—for a larger allocation of national resources. The political center was held predominantly by Ashkenazim, who dominated the main elements of society: its politics, the military, and business. All this began to change in 1977 when the Likud Party and its large Sephardi constituency assumed power for the first time. Gradually, power ebbed away from the old elite and toward the newcomers. This process gained momentum in the 1990s, by which time the Askenazim and the Sephardim were struggling not only over power and resources but also over the very nature of the society itself. By the end of the 1990s, groups that were once at the periphery of Israeli society—Sephardim and many religious Jews—could make a reasonable claim that they were at the "center."

The position of the Arab population within Israel also was challenged in the 1990s. Through much of the decade, Arabs as a whole improved their economic lot, in large part through active government policy. The Rabin government, in particular, explicitly tried to narrow the income gap between Jews and Arabs by increasing government support for the Arab educational system and the Arab share of public income transfers. As this process unfolded, mainstream Jewish opinion moved away from the far-right conception (and fear) of Israeli Arabs as a "fifth column" and more toward a belief that coexistence, albeit within a Jewish state, was possible. Opinion abruptly shifted back in October 2000, when some Arabs engaged in violent clashes with the government, police, and Jewish commuters after the Palestinians launched the new Intifada in the occupied territories. The violent reactions against Jewish communities in the north of Israel that forced the closure of the main Wadi Ara road, cutting off a major link between the Galilee area and the rest of the country, was especially disturbing in the eyes of many Israeli Jews.

For Arabs, the police's aggressive response, including live fire that caused the deaths of some of the protesters, bred resentment and renewed deep-seated grievances against the Israeli government. Following the riots, the government appointed a Commission of Inquiry, headed by Supreme Court

Judge Benjamin Orr. As has been evident throughout the commission's investigation, the events of October 2000 frustrated the earlier hope that the Jewish-Arab schism could be moderated.

One of the fundamental characteristics of the state of Israel is that it is a democratic Jewish state. However, as was apparent from the outset, there is an inherent contradiction between the nation's two core values. The attempt, as set out in the Declaration of Independence, to create both equality for all citizens (including non-Jews) and a state imbued with Jewish values, symbols, and practices, therefore, was always destined to be contradictory. In the 1990s, the contradiction was exposed—more than ever—and the defined nature of the state was challenged. In a well-known Supreme Court case involving the Jewish community of Katzir, the court ruled that the government could no longer allocate land to its citizens based on their religion or ethnicity and could no longer prevent Arab citizens from living where they chose.[29] Prior to the court's landmark decision, the sale of land to Arabs had been heavily restricted out of concern for security and demographics.

It is not surprising that the heightened collision between Jewish and democratic values has raised many questions about the nature and future of the country. These have ranged from definitions of "who is a Jew?" to land-rights issues and critical questions over the sources of law and power in the country. The answers to these very critical dilemmas hit hard at any experiment in pluralism. Indeed, the whole raison d'être of the state was being confronted throughout the 1990s. These dilemmas fueled in ethnic groups feelings of political alienation from the national center. Significantly, this alienation was felt not only in the Arab sector but also among groups in the Jewish population (particularly the Haredim).

The political setting was also shaken during the decade as result of the ongoing swing between left- and right-wing coalition governments, which created political instability and fueled ethnic differences. Israel became stuck in a political stalemate between the two main parties, Labor (with its traditional Ashkenazi-tilted composition) and Likud (with its large Sephardi constituency). Neither party was ever strong enough to govern alone, and to overcome the other, each needed the support of smaller "kingpin" parties. The result was a compromise on ideological issues, as both Likud and Labor had to make concessions to garner support from smaller parties. Despite these compromises, political stability was elusive, and structural changes to the political system were prescribed. The resulting introduction of direct elections for the prime minister did not produce the desired effect of diminishing the role of the smaller parties (indeed, it can be argued that it had the opposite effect), and this "reform" has since been revoked. To us, this experience strongly indicates that cosmetic changes to the political system are too superficial to promote political stability. Indeed, such changes are doomed to failure. The roots of Israel's political instability emanate from its ethnic makeup and the schisms within its society. As such, political stability can only be achieved by addressing—and, we hope, narrowing—the divisions directly.

Indeed, one of the major political lessons of the 1990s is that each of Israel's major political groupings had to learn to acknowledge the limits of its ability to dictate solutions. At no stage was one party or faction strong enough to rule without coalition; all had to learn the necessity of living together. The need for compromise created a handing out of power and resources. Typically, the smaller kingpin parties would demand the diversion of extra state funds toward their constituents in return for their support of the largest party's platform. The rise of Shas, the Sephardi-Haredi party, is paradigmatic: Shas remained in the government for most of the 1990s, while Likud and Labor regularly switched places as the governing and main opposition parties. As a result, Shas managed to achieve (in both Likud- and Labor-led governments) large transfers of funds toward its school and welfare systems. But the exercise of raw political power in this fashion can create a backlash. One indication that this has already occurred in Israel is the political success in 1999 of the anti-religious Shinui Party, which campaigned on a platform against the "overtaking of government by the Haredim."

Lest we conclude on too pessimistic a note, it is important to note a number of successes in the 1990s. The most significant success was the absorption of the nearly 1 million immigrants from the former Soviet Union, an event that led to a 20 percent increase in the population of the country. That this occurred as smoothly as it did (with bumps along the way, to be sure) is a testament to the continued power of the idea that prompted the creation of the modern state of Israel as a refuge for Jews from all parts of the world, regardless of need, race, or ethnic identity. The United States also assisted in the absorption process by providing a $10 billion loan guarantee to the government. In narrow economic terms, the Soviet immigration also can be judged highly successful. Despite initial concerns about the employability of many of the immigrants, the Israeli economy absorbed large numbers within a relatively short period, generating a reduction in the overall unemployment from 12 percent at the beginning of the decade to roughly 6 percent near the end (a level lower than that of most Western European countries).

Israel's other major success in the 1990s, especially during the latter half, was the outstanding performance of its high-tech sector, with many foreign companies, especially from the United States, investing in Israeli business. Undoubtedly, the region's relative geopolitical calm helped to allay the fears of foreign investors. Although Israel's hi-tech sector has been caught in the worldwide downdraft in that sector that began in 2000, Israeli high-tech companies are still more than holding their own. They would do better, of course, if the security situation improved, and in any event will do better as the world economy recovers from the recession that began some time in 2001.

In sum, the 1990s represented a dramatic decade for Israel. It was during this period that the country seemed to mature from adolescence, abandon some of its illusory aspirations, and begin to debate its future.

Challenges Ahead

If the definition of a successful pluralistic society is providing the minimum amount of social cohesion sufficient to allow many of its citizens self-expression and opportunities for economic advancement, while tolerating the diverse views and values of others, then Israel has been reasonably successful—so far. There certainly is no lack of self-expression in Israel, where the typical citizen is outspoken on a full range of issues—social, religious, and political. Many Israelis have enjoyed an extraordinary increase in their standard of living, especially those equipped with advanced skills. Many others, though, continue to lag behind, as is the case both with Sephardim and with Arabs. Even more troubling, Israel is far from a fully tolerant society. There are deep ethnic divides and even deeper schisms between secular and religious Jews.

Nonetheless, the institutions surveyed in this chapter have provided enough social glue to impart values and an understanding of history, in order to achieve a reasonable degree of social cohesion. The critical question ahead for the country is whether the institutions it has successfully made use of in the past will be sufficient to ensure social and political stability in the future. The continued presence, if not the widening, of the schisms outlined in chapter 3 pose particularly difficult challenges, aggravated by the likely demographic arithmetic.

In contrast with Europe, Japan, and the United States, Israel today has a remarkably young population. These intercountry disparities will continue to grow in the future, as the populations of both Europe and America continue to age rapidly. What will this now young country look like in the years ahead, as it enlarges and possibly ages along the lines described in chapter 3? Now that the Russian immigration is more or less at an end, how will Israel cope with the fact that a steadily rising share of its population will be Arab? As violence between Palestinians and Jews continues, Jewish immigration from other countries does not look promising, while Jewish *emigration* (especially of highly trained Israelis who can easily find work in the West) is likely to grow. This adds up to a demographic bomb threat for Israel, one whose fuse was lengthened, perhaps by several decades, when the former Soviet immigrants arrived but is now considerably shorter.

There is no assurance that a peaceful resolution of the Palestinian question, which would be a desirable outcome, would necessarily dispel tensions between Israeli Arabs and Jews. In fact, it is possible that, after such a rapprochement, Arab Israelis would intensify their demands that the state of Israel be transformed, de jure and de facto, into the "state of all its citizens" and thereby abandon the Zionist ethos on which the nation was founded. Some Israelis already support a move in this direction, which at least one Israeli analyst has suggested is quickly becoming a reality.[30]

Whatever the outcome may be on the Palestinian front, the Israeli government must decide what immigration policy to follow in the future. In particular, will the Law of Return, which grants automatic citizenship to all Jews, continue to be the law of the land, and if so, who will determine the parameters of what it means to "be Jewish" for this purpose? A related question is what rules, secular or religious, will govern the possible conversion of tens, if not hundreds, of thousands of Russian immigrants? With the recent upsurge in support for Haredi parties, it is unlikely that the current policy, which vests all power for answering these questions in religious bodies, will change. But continuation of this policy will aggravate relations between Israel and many American Jews, who resent the rejection of non-Orthodox Jewish religious movements.

In fact, of all the schisms discussed in this chapter, the one that poses the most serious threat to the cohesion of Israeli society (at least its Jewish component) is the growing divide between secular and religious Jews. In contrast to other tensions that may be moderated, if not eliminated by the narrowing of socioeconomic gaps, this is not the case with the religious-secular schism, which at its core, is an ideological struggle backed by political power. At the extreme, the rule of law could be under threat. Haredim believe that Jewish religious law (*Halacha*)—a binding set of laws by which Orthodox Jews live their lives—must govern the lives of *all* Israelis. Civil law *is* religious law, and vice versa, to the Haredi way of thinking. This mode of thought is anathema to the majority of Israeli Jews, who are secular. As we have noted, the rise of the Shinui Party in the 1999 elections, with its gain of six seats in the Knesset, was fueled largely by the public's growing opposition to Haredi ideas.

In short, the emotions over the religious-secular schism run very deep, much deeper than the schisms between Sephardim and Ashkenazim, which, over time, are becoming blurred by intermarriage. This is not likely to be true for secular and Haredi Jews. Finding ways—at least minimal measures to begin with—to bridge some of the religious-secular divide should be paramount on the Israeli national agenda. In the next chapter, we offer suggestions for meeting this challenge.

CHAPTER FIVE

Meeting Israel's Future Challenges

T HE MELTING POT ethos in Israel is essentially gone, replaced by an uneasy pluralism. This paradigmatic shift—evident first and perhaps most dramatically in 1977 when the Likud ascended to political power—is likely to persist for the foreseeable future. The institutions and policies surveyed in the previous chapter are broadly designed to accommodate the transition toward pluralism, and, to a certain degree, they have worked. Israel can be rightly proud, for example, of its economic, scientific, and technical achievements, accomplished under conditions unlike those faced by other countries. What other nation, for example, has voluntarily welcomed immigrants totaling almost 20 percent of the initial population in the span of only a few years and at the same time enjoyed faster real growth than that experienced by the world's leading economic power, the United States? This is what happened in Israel in the first half of the 1990s.

Over the long run, however, Israel's deep and growing ethnic and religious divisions, compounded by wide and growing economic inequality among some segments of the population, cannot be healthy for the country's economic future or even for its military security. The security wolf at the door reminds Israeli Jews that, however deep their differences might be, a worse fate awaits them if they allow their divisions to disable their ability to defend themselves. Nevertheless, the growing divisions among Israelis pose security dangers in and of themselves. An army of men and women who have little in common with one another will find it increasingly difficult to fight shoulder to shoulder against hostile forces facing the country.

At some point—we hope earlier rather than later—the security challenges to Israel will recede. The Palestinian problem that seems so intractable now may be susceptible to solution—if not a warm peace, then perhaps an armistice. Once that day arrives, however, the divisions we discuss in this book are likely to take center stage. Indeed, it is possible that these internal problems, which we believe lie at the core of Israel's own national identity, will not wait for Israel's security challenges to diminish.[1] Unless something is done to reverse the process, the rift between secular and religious Jews almost certainly will continue to widen. Arguably, the same will be true for divisions between Arabs and Jews, as well as for the ethnic and economic splits among Israeli Jews.

What can be done in the meantime to arrest these trends? How can a national discourse about the need to reinforce a stable pluralistic society be promoted? With all due humility, we hope this short monograph can make a meaningful contribution simply by calling attention to the challenge. But clearly much more is required. Political and religious leaders must put the challenge of maintaining national cohesion, which is discussed now among individuals in the privacy of their homes or workplaces, near the top of the nation's social and political agenda.

Of course, much more than an airing of different opinions is required. Concrete actions, including reforms of existing institutions, changes in laws, and the like, must be identified and taken. In this chapter, we offer some tentative thoughts on what steps might help. Some of the suggestions may be controversial, but given the severity of the internal challenges we have outlined, we believe that bold and creative solutions are required. At the very least, we hope to stimulate a healthy debate over what measures and institutions are needed to maintain Israel's experiment in pluralism.

Unity and Disunity in Israeli Society

Before turning to our specific policy suggestions, we need to underscore the difficulty of the challenge, which is complicated by two conflicting trends that uneasily coexist today in Israeli society: one toward the empowerment of separate sociocultural and political groups (abetted by government financial support), the other toward the blurring of some of the distinctions between groups (which could be encouraged by the combination of demographic trends and limited resources). In short, there are forces that simultaneously are pulling Israelis together and apart, within and across each of the major groups we have described. How all of this will play out is very difficult to predict.

Consider, for example, the expansion of the Ashkenazi-Haredi population. As their numbers grow, it may be impossible for Haredim to continue having their male members study rather than work until the age of thirty or more. Budgetary pressures eventually may force change, with younger Haredim entering the labor force. This could prove beneficial, since it would help to integrate Haredim into the rest of Israeli society.

Immigrants from the Soviet Union are also gradually, although partially, integrating into the prevailing Israeli culture. At the same time, many of these immigrants continue to cling to the culture, language, and other institutions they left behind. Separatist tendencies are even more apparent among the Arab population, where demands for more autonomy continue to grow (especially in the wake of the Intifada).

Nonetheless, it would be wrong to conclude that Israel consists of multiple ethnic, religious, and cultural islands, widely separated from each other. The reality is that most Israelis do not live—or think of themselves as living—in cloistered enclaves. Nor do most of their leaders think and behave this way. The forces that tie them together are strong; among them are army service and daily security issues. But there is also a more prosaic factor: Israel is a small country where geographic closeness inevitably compels individuals from different groups to rub shoulders with each other virtually daily.

But rubbing shoulders does not mean agreement. With the gradual collapse of the hegemonic political culture—a change that became visible after the Likud came to power in 1977—wide differences over values, rules of behavior, and cultural myths have emerged and should persist.

Consider, for example, the ongoing controversy over the Law of Return, which remains on the public agenda. Many immigrants from the Soviet Union who are not Jewish understandably are unsympathetic with the views of the increasingly powerful Ultra-Orthodox, who oppose any efforts to remove religious control over the definition of who is a Jew, let alone amendments to the Law of Return that liberalize immigration criteria. At this writing, no resolution of this conflict seems to be in sight. Or take the related controversy aroused by the demand of many Israelis for more widely available non-Orthodox religious services, a view shared by many Jews in the Diaspora. Unless some creative solution to this issue can be found—one that satisfies both Orthodox and non-Orthodox inside and outside Israel—it will not be surprising to see growing tension between American Jews (the large majority of whom are not Orthodox) and the state of Israel. More broadly, if the Ultra-Orthodox continue to press their views on the rest of Israeli society, they will provoke equally extreme, secular, views in reaction. There is a real danger that this gulf will continue to widen in the future.

There are also conflicting pressures within the religious community itself. Many religious Jews are becoming more secular and adopting so-called modern ways of life.[2] At the same time, other religious Jews have moved in the opposite direction, toward the strict Ashkenazi-Haredi religious customs and rituals. The rise of the Shas Party, and its establishment of alternative cultural, social, and educational institutions, illustrates the attraction of this latter tendency.[3]

Of course, the mere rise of separate enclaves—whether based on religion, ethnic origin, or race—need not aggravate social tensions. In fact, sometimes the formation of collective identities can strengthen individuals and subgroups and ease societal pressures overall.[4] But this positive outcome is likely only if members of these separate groups do not insist on imposing their values and way of life on the rest of society. The Supreme Court plays a major role in ensuring that they do not succeed in such an endeavor. Yet true social cohesion requires that the members of various groups internalize tolerance toward others with different points of view. Israel has some way to go before this characteristic of pluralism is truly achieved.

Political Tension and Its Ethnic Context

The challenge of maintaining pluralism in Israel is further complicated by the close relationship between the political alignments of certain groups within society and their views about Israel's national security—specifically, the country's policies toward its Arab neighbors and the Palestinians.

In brief, the Israeli electorate is sharply divided into two camps of similar size with respect to issues of security and peace. This division has had daily implications for public life, especially in recent decades. In conventional American terms, one might use the concepts of "hawks" and "doves" to reflect the views of the two camps.[5] During the 2001 election campaign, for example, both major parties flew the dual flag of "Peace" and "Security," the main difference between them being the order in which the two words appeared. Nonetheless, the split in the public debate on this subject is much deeper than implied by this minor difference in political slogans.

The relationship between the division on security matters and attitudes toward pluralism is illustrated in ongoing public polls, such as the Peace Index conducted by a research group at Tel Aviv University and published monthly by a major newspaper.[6] Although the public's attitude toward these questions obviously fluctuates with the number and intensity of violent episodes, the polls show several stable patterns that relate to the subject of this book. In these polls, the religious sector within the Jewish population consistently and clearly expresses hawkish views, although the composition of this camp and the complexion of its views are diverse. The majority tend to be hawkish for ideological reasons—that is, to achieve a Greater Israel, including the territories held by Israel since the 1967 Six-Day War. Indeed, the radical elements of the religious camp would even risk war to preserve full control of these territories.

A smaller group within the religious sector—the Sephardi-Haredi party Shas—is unique in that, while its members are considered hawkish for practical (not necessarily ideological) reasons, the leader of this theocratic party, who also dictates the positions of the party's delegates to the Knesset and the government, occasionally has sounded more like a dove (although this has changed since the Intifada). On these occasions, Shas explains that the value of peace (provided that it meets security needs) takes precedence over the goal of territorial integrity. A similar pattern may be observed among Ashkenazi-Haredim. Still, only a rather small group among the mainstream religious population put more emphasis on peace than on territorial considerations.

Among secular Jews, polls report strong dovish views, but it is not clear whether these reflect a secular world view or the influence of other and more prosaic traits such as differences in schooling, occupation, and income from those in the religious camp. Another explanation for the more dovish attitudes among secular Jews may be that more of them are Ashkenazim than Sephardim. Therefore, the dovish tendency of secular Jews as a whole may reflect, in part, the political-security preferences of Ashkenazim, a tendency that, in turn, is correlated with social-economic class.

The polling data report no clear patterns among immigrants from the former Soviet Union. But judging from statements of leaders of the immigrants' two parties and the positions they take in debates in the Knesset and the government, these immigrants evidently lean toward the hawkish camp.[7]

In sum, there appears to be some correlation between ethnicity and attitudes toward peace and security.[8] Because security is more important in Israel than in other countries, divisions over it tend to aggravate or reinforce ethnic and secular-religious divisions. If this is true, then the resolution of tensions with the Palestinians should tend to ease ethnic tensions among Jews.

But the opposite outcome also could emerge. With peace in hand—or even the mere prospect of peace—the suppressed tensions among various Jewish groups may be released. The adverse effects of the political debate surfaced in the 1990s when the assassination of Prime Minister Yitzhak Rabin opened a wound that refuses to heal and is still raw in the Israeli psyche. It bears emphasis that the assassination took place in a climate of bitter struggle among Jews between proponents and opponents of the Oslo accords—between doves and hawks. In particular, some from the left overtly accused the right of creating the climate that led to the assassination. Although this view was not widely shared, it contributed to political tensions.

Related to the security issue is the fact that Jews who live in settlements outside the Green Line have been living under increasing tension since the Al-Aqsa uprising. Many, if not most, inhabitants of these settlements belong to the religious camp and consider themselves victims of the Oslo accords. These individuals, whose routine activities have been disrupted to such an extent in the course of the unrest that even travel within and between communities has become life threatening, have numerous relatives and friends in religious circles inside Israel proper. As a result, the ongoing security risks outside Israel spill over inside the country and thus contribute to the estrangement of some religious Jews from secular Jews.

The practical lesson we draw from all of this is that, if Israel's political leaders could ease their rhetoric over security matters without blurring the deep differences in substance, they could help to heal some of the raw wounds and divisions that separate Jews of different ethnic and religious backgrounds. This is likely to be true even at a time when the country otherwise has come together—at least temporarily—in reaction to the daily security threat posed by Palestinian radicals.

Of course, we also believe that more substantive steps—beyond rhetoric—can be taken to heal some of Israel's divisions. As we cautioned at the outset, these suggestions are both tentative and controversial, but we turn to them next nonetheless.

Arab-Jewish Relations

The deepest divide within Israel is between Arabs and Jews. Given the long history of this "uneasy" (to use an understatement) relationship, the best that can be hoped for in the near future is some gradual move—on both sides—toward greater toleration of the other. In the long run, Israel has no other choice. The Arabs will continue to be an integral, and indeed growing, part of Israel's population.

Policies toward Arab-Jewish relations can be arrayed on a spectrum, depending on the degree of integration that is desired by both sides. A minimalist objective would be to continue what is, in effect, a "cold peace." In this scenario, Arabs and Jews continue to live and work separately. Personal contacts are kept to a minimum. The aim is simply to avoid violent outbreaks.

Advocates of a minimalist approach to Arab-Jewish relations—a continuation of the policy of "separateness"—presumably would argue that more aggressive steps to promote integration of Arab citizens in Israeli society would not diminish Arab sympathies with the Palestinian cause and, in the end, would fail because Arabs do not want to integrate.[9] Nonetheless, we believe there is a case for a more ambitious view, one that seeks to rectify the economic and legal inequities between the Arab and Jewish populations. This view rests on three counterpropositions. One is that the pessimists may simply be wrong in claiming that Arab attitudes are immune to economic conditions. There is no proof that improvements in economic status—more aid to Arab educational facilities, steps to end discrimination in labor markets—would fail to soften the Arab suspicion of, and in some quarters contempt for, their Israeli counterparts. The fact is that such a comprehensive integrationist strategy has never been tried.

The second argument for the more ambitious view claims that, if more is not done soon to help the Arab community, Arab citizens will become even more estranged from the rest of Israel and, in the process, will become an even greater security threat than they may be now. A third argument is a moral one. How can an Israeli majority continue to justify a "separate but *not* equal" policy for a population of more than 1 million (and growing) Arabs?

The major justification for maintaining the more extreme view of separation, which appears to be implicit Israeli policy, is that anything else poses an unacceptable security risk to the Jewish majority: if Arabs are more integrated into Israeli society, Israel may expose itself even more to acts of sabotage and violence. But in the long run, there are also security risks in maintaining a policy of separateness, which reinforces feelings of grievance now deeply felt within the Arab community. This point is underscored by the demographic trends outlined in chapter 3. Arabs will steadily comprise a larger share of the Israeli population.

On balance, therefore, to us the arguments favoring an integrationist policy—or at least attempting to introduce one to see if it works—more than counterbalance the arguments against it. We understand the political risks of adopting such an approach in the tense political environment in which this book was written (2001). But we hope that eventually the time will come when more concrete measures can be taken.

What might these steps be? One place to begin is for the Israeli public and leaders to learn a lesson from the country's own immigrant absorption experience, which underscores the importance of a common language as a unifying institution. The hard fact is that, for Israeli Arabs to improve their chances in the labor market, they need to acquire a fair degree of fluency in Hebrew. Therefore, at a minimum, Hebrew language skills need to be taught and studied much earlier in Arab schools than is now the case.

Conversely, if Israelis are to develop some empathy with the Arab community, Jewish children should learn Arabic at an early age as well. We realize that this may be difficult to accomplish when Israeli children are also studying English, as they must if they want to be integrated into the rest of the world. But the problems between Arabs and Jews are sufficiently serious—and likely to be that way for some time—that one place to begin is for Jewish children at least to have a better appreciation of Arab culture and language.

Another important step that Israel must take is to devote more resources to infrastructure development within Arab communities. This means spending more on roads, educational facilities, and public works. The current disparities in infrastructure between Arabs and Jews, which contribute to disparities in both the level and growth of income between the two, are painfully obvious and eventually must be addressed.

Narrowing the Secular-Religious Divide

What may be hard for those outside Israel to appreciate fully is that bridging the gap between secular and religious Jews is likely to be very difficult—almost as difficult as bridging the Arab-Jewish divide. At the core of religious-secular tension is a continuing controversy over the appropriate role for religion in state affairs. This tension exists even in a country like the United States, which prides itself on the separation between religion and state and indeed embodies that separation in its constitution. The tension is much more evident in a country like modern Israel, which was founded as a Zionist state, a homeland for Jews. As long as Israel is to be a *Jewish* state, then some role for religion in governing the affairs of the people is naturally to be expected.

The debate within Israel is over how much of a role. Broadly speaking, secular Jews are comfortable retaining the Zionist ethos of the state, but many want to end the government's deference to religious authorities in the realm of civil affairs. For religious Jews, abandoning religious law where it now governs would represent an abdication of much of what Israel represents. This difference in views is so deep and so fundamental that, for all intents and purposes, it seems irreconcilable and may well be.

The religious-secular divide within Israel is complicated by the divisions over the Law of Return and the question "Who is a Jew?", which is discussed in chapter 2. As we observe there, resolving this question is as important, and possibly even more important, for Jews in the Diaspora as for Jews in Israel. We have no magic bullet for narrowing this divide. It cannot be done on its own terms. Religious Jews will continue to believe what they believe, and so will secular Jews.

The example of the United States, or a version of it, nonetheless serves as a possible long-run model for Israel: a society that tolerates religious diversity but takes religion out of state affairs. Israel's version would be to minimize the state's intervention. In our view, secular Jews would not be nearly as upset over matters of religion if deeply religious Jews governed their own civil affairs (the rules governing marriage, divorce, burial, and so forth) but did not impose their religious views on the rest of the state, which, after all, remains overwhelmingly secular. One other sociolegal reform needed is to enable civil marriage in cases where religious marriage is not possible. At the same time, religious Jews perhaps would be more tolerant of secular society if secular Jews were more tolerant of them. In short, more of a "live and let live" attitude, which is the hallmark of pluralism, would go a long way toward easing tensions between the two communities.

One possible method for accomplishing this objective, with specific regard to the separate Haredi social systems, would perhaps be the following compact: the government would guarantee continued financial support for Haredi educational and social service institutions in return for commitments to introduce a core curriculum of secular (nonreligious) topics, such as mathematics and civics courses on democracy, in which Haredi students would demonstrate their proficiency. In addition, Haredi students, on graduation, would fulfill some type of compulsory service, either military or civilian (discussed in greater detail shortly).

Some within each community will say that such a compromise is impossible, at least in the current environment. But we believe that it contains the seeds of an idea that could begin to ease some of the tension that now exists between the groups, which we believe poses the greatest danger to Israeli cohesiveness outside the deep differences between Israeli Jews and Arabs.

Narrowing Israel's Educational Divide

There is no turning back from the transition away from a melting pot ethos and toward an acceptance of choice and pluralism as a key foundation of the Israeli educational system. Nonetheless, Israel faces two key educational challenges going forward.

One challenge is to impart a minimum set of shared values and knowledge to each new generation. All nations must meet this challenge, but it is especially daunting in Israel, given the wide religious and ethnic gulfs that exist within the country. Indeed, for some time Israelis have been debating what it means to be an Israeli—an existential question whose answer determines how the country's children are educated and thus what Israeli society will look like in the future. Should Israelis be educated to be citizens of a state governed by or derived from *Halacha*, the Jewish religious law? Or should they be educated to be citizens of a state infused with Zionist ideology and Jewish culture and religion, but nonetheless tolerant of Orthodox and non-Orthodox Jews, Arabs, Christians, and those of other faiths and national backgrounds? Reflecting the religious-secular divide in the country, a minority of Israeli Jews share the first vision, while the majority share the second.

What is a society to do about educating its children when there is a deep, fundamental split among its population about such a basic issue? In the 1990s, the Israeli government established two separate commissions to examine curricula in the schools. Their findings point to a constructive set of parallel recommendations, which may help to address this challenge. On the one hand, the Shenhar Commission found a noticeable lack of emphasis in state secular schools on Jewish traditions and culture.[10] On the other hand, the Kremnitzer Commission found that all schools—

religious schools in particular—could strengthen their teaching of the importance of democratic values, including tolerance of different points of view.[11] In our view, Israeli schools could benefit from the application of *both* sets of recommendations: more teaching of Jewish culture and religious practices in the secular schools, coupled with a greater role for teaching about a democratic and humanistic way of life in the religious schools. Perhaps then students in each system would have a greater appreciation for the values of the other, which they would retain as adults.

The other educational challenge is to ensure that all schools provide as many students as possible with the necessary training and zest for continued learning so that they are easily integrated in the labor market and larger society when they reach adulthood.[12] Meeting this challenge is not difficult for schools with students from families with incomes in the middle and upper segments of the income distribution. These schools have the resources to provide adequate training, and the students who attend them are likely to have home lives conducive to furthering their education. The main educational challenges are present in both Arab and Jewish schools attended primarily by children from lower-income families, where resources are often less than adequate and where family life at home may not support education and learning.

To be sure, money alone will not cure educational disparities. Evidence from the United States is mixed as to whether greater financial resources translate into better student performance.[13] Similarly, economic studies have documented significant inefficiencies in Israeli schools attended by Jewish children, implying a weak connection between money and educational performance.[14] At the same time, however, the funding disparity between schools attended by Arab and Jewish students is evident to the naked eye. It is difficult to believe that the relative performance of Arab students has not been adversely affected. As a result, we recommend a reallocation of resources toward Israeli schools with students—whether Arab or Jewish—from poorer socioeconomic backgrounds as a necessary, but not sufficient, condition for ensuring more equal educational opportunities.[15]

Educational opportunity is not just a matter of equity. The Israeli economy has been as successful as it has been largely because of the country's large number of highly trained and motivated workers—what economists like to call human capital. In the 1990s, Israel imported some of these skills through the wave of immigrants from the former Soviet Union. In the future, Israel will have to replenish and augment its own human capital, as immigration almost certainly will diminish. As a purely economic proposition, the country will be wasting its potential comparative advantage—the skills of its people—if it does not do all it can to ensure that children from all backgrounds have a fair shot at developing those skills.

Narrowing Economic Gaps

Israel has a comprehensive system of public services—in education and health, among other arenas—that aims to improve the living standards of the entire population. Social spending also tends to reduce social inequality and to narrow disparities among groups. As described in previous chapters, the dividing lines in incomes and standards of living tend to coincide with ethnic divides: between Jews and Arabs, between Jews of Asian-African origin versus those of European-American origin, and so on. It is reasonable to assume that economic inequality exacerbates ethnic tensions. By implication, one of the most important ways to ease ethnic tensions is to narrow social and economic disparities.

This is a real challenge because income distribution is highly inequitable in Israel. In this sense, Israel competes with the United States for the bottom ranking among developed Western countries. In the mid-1990s, according to the Israel National Insurance Institute, the Gini index for inequality in net income (household income after transfers and taxes) was 0.35 in Israel. Among the countries shown in table 5-1, only the United States looked worse, with a higher Gini index and thus even greater inequality.[16] These two countries also fared poorly in their measures of poverty. In both Israel and the United States, 18 percent of the population is mired in relative poverty. (In most countries, the accepted notion of poverty is relative, and the definition of the poverty line is half the median national income.)

We want to underscore that these data refer to disposable income, which takes account of both taxes paid and transfers received from the government. If one looks solely at *earned income*, the Gini inequality index is

Table 5-1. Incidence of Poverty and the Gini Index of Disposable Income in the 1990s

Country and year	Percentage in poverty	Gini index
United States (1997)	17.9	0.38
Israel (1997)	17.7	0.35
Italy (1995)	12.6	0.34
Australia (1994)	12.7	0.32
Germany (1994)	12.0	0.30
France (1994)	8.4	0.29
Canada (1994)	11.2	0.29
Holland (1994)	8.4	0.27
Belgium (1996)	8.0	0.27
Luxembourg (1994)	4.5	0.24
Norway (1995)	6.0	0.23
Sweden (1995)	8.8	0.22

Source: National Insurance Institute, *Annual Survey 2000* (Jerusalem: National Insurance Institute, March 2001).

0.52. Thus inequality would be far worse in Israel without active government help to offset it.

Of even greater concern in Israel is that earned income inequality has worsened perceptibly in the past two decades. The downslide began in the 1980s, a decade marked by hyperinflation followed by a successful stabilization program. During that period, the Gini index for earned income rose from 0.43 to 0.47 (see table 5-2). The situation grew even worse in the 1990s, rising to 0.52 by the end of the decade. Government intervention also was more successful in reducing income inequality in the 1980s, when the Gini index for disposable income was 0.32. By the end of the 1990s, this measure had risen to 0.36.[17]

It is important to focus on some further complexities in Israel's income distribution. Although Israel's poverty rate is about 18 percent nationwide, it is 42 percent among the Arab population. There is no doubt that differences in education and infrastructure contribute to this disparity, which is one of the reasons we call for more investment in the Arab sector. But there is poverty among Israeli Jews as well, especially among Haredi Jews who live in Bnei Barak and Jerusalem, many of whom have with-

Table 5-2. Israel's Gini Index before and after Taxes and Transfers, 1979–99

Year	Before taxes and transfers	After taxes and transfers
1979	0.4318	0.3181
1980	0.4337	0.3239
1981	0.4390	0.3185
1982	0.4441	0.3122
1983	0.4392	0.3005
1984	0.4723	0.3267
1985	0.4678	0.3119
1988	0.4574	0.3221
1989	0.4741	0.3252
1990	0.4799	0.3263
1991	0.4901	0.3272
1992	0.4977	0.3391
1993	0.4940	0.3290
1994	0.5019	0.3441
1995	0.4971	0.3365
1996	0.4956	0.3285
1997	0.5045	0.3332
1997[a]	0.5085	0.3531
1998[a]	0.5119	0.3523
1999[a]	0.5167	0.3593

Source: National Insurance Institute, *Annual Survey 2000* (Jerusalem: National Insurance Institute, March 2001).
a. Revised sample.

drawn from the labor force. Similarly, the incidence of poverty is perceptibly higher in places populated by the descendants of immigrants from Asia and Africa who came to Israel in the 1950s.

Paralleling the problems of income inequality are the disparities among groups in unemployment. Roughly speaking, the same groups that have low average incomes also tend to have disproportionately high rates of unemployment.

In the past, the government attempted to narrow regional economic disparities through subsidies and grants of economic benefits to populations in peripheral areas. As it has turned out, many towns in the periphery—but, fortunately, not all—have failed to prosper and have been left behind by the economic boom enjoyed in the country's main urban areas. Notable exceptions include the development towns of Yoqne'am and Migdal ha-'Emeq, which have become prosperous mainly for two reasons: successful socioeconomic integration of immigrants from Russia and attraction of entrepreneurial business activity, especially in high-tech industries. Still, as a general proposition, Israel's regional policy has not been an effective means of reducing income disparities—both in principle and by design.

The more productive course, for Israel as for other countries, is to view improvements in education as the key to economic success, both for individuals and for social equality. That is the main reason we suggest a more equitable system of supporting schools populated disproportionately by children from disadvantaged families in an effort to narrow the disparities.

The political problem is that educational remedies promise effective results only over the long run. What about the shorter run, or the time horizon of most political authorities? Here, the best answer lies in a macroeconomic policy that gives somewhat greater weight to encouraging growth than to containing inflation.[18] It is possible that more effective enforcement of Israel's minimum wage law might help somewhat in assuring greater equality (although debate over the efficacy of minimum wage laws continues in both Israel and the United States).

Another effective short-run solution for remedying income inequalities lies in tax reform. As it is now, Israel offers far-reaching tax exemptions that severely narrow the tax base. Thus, while the country's income tax system is progressive, the nation still relies heavily on sales taxes—half of revenues are generated in this fashion—and also funds its social security system through a separate tax on labor. In combination, both direct taxes and social security taxes reduce the overall progressivity of the tax system. In principle, the overall tax system could be made more progressive by cutting back the current income tax exemptions and lowering rates, much as the United States did in the 1980s (but has since partially undone). Lower tax rates should improve income tax compliance and enforcement, which in Israel leave much to be desired. With better compliance, income tax revenues would climb and make it possible for Israel to reduce its reliance on regressive direct taxes.

Immigration Policy

Israel has one of the most elaborate sets of policies anywhere in the world for integrating immigrants into the mainstream of society. Moreover, Israel's absorption policies have proved to be adaptable. One of the initial mistakes was to send the new immigrants to places not of their own choice. This policy led to some very important achievements, but it also caused a great deal of resentment and alienation on the part of the new immigrants. Later, the policy switched to allowing immigrants a choice of where they wanted to live and work, a result that is widely seen as more humane and effective. Most immigrants have located where they desire, but in many cases they have not yet integrated into society. Therefore, a challenge still exists for both the host population and immigrants to find ways to interact more positively and to advance societal cohesion, while maintaining individual or group values and preferences.

One specific immigration-related issue that can and should receive attention in the future concerns the current Israeli policy toward guest workers. As noted in chapter 2, more than 250,000 guest workers are living temporarily within Israel, largely doing the construction and agricultural work formerly performed by Palestinians. As in Europe, these guest workers are not integrated into the rest of Israeli society, they are not treated as regular residents, and their living standards are well below those of the average Israeli (even the average Arab Israeli).[19] To say the least, this is not a healthy state of affairs, especially if, as is likely, the government encourages even greater reliance on guest workers. As the numbers of these workers increase, the more difficult it will be, as a practical matter, to ignore their plight. Israel eventually must choose between four very different approaches on this question.

In theory, Israel could extend similar absorption policies—extensive Hebrew language training, housing, and other types of assistance—with the aim of eventually extending citizenship to guest workers. The major argument for such a policy is that it would be the humane thing to do, especially for workers who are permitted to stay for lengthy periods (constantly renewing their visas). The obvious drawback is that any increase in the non-Jewish population threatens the cohesiveness of the state and potentially adds sociopolitical complications to those Israel already confronts with its diverse citizenry.

A second option would be to admit guest workers, but only for a limited period—say no more than two to three years—and not increase their overall numbers. In effect, such a policy would ensure the status quo, while avoiding much, if not all, of the problems associated with the long-term residence of existing guest workers. The main advantage is that this approach would avoid the absorption dilemmas associated with graduation toward citizenship, while retaining a source of low-cost labor, with its associated economic benefits for Israeli firms and ultimately Israeli consumers. The key disadvantage, however, is that as long as guest workers continue to live in substandard conditions—which is inevitable unless the government subsidizes their living costs, an option that does not appear politically feasible—Israel will continue to have a moral blot on its political and social system.

The third course is to phase out the guest worker program. This would solve the absorption problem and facilitate the objective of maintaining a cohesive society. But it would be costly, since, in the absence of guest workers, Israeli farmers and construction companies would have to bid up wages substantially in order to attract native Israelis—both Jews and Arabs—to take their place. Of course, with higher wages, some agricultural production and construction would no longer be profitable, so there would be a cutback in these activities (more in agriculture than in construction). Assuming that some significant fraction of the 250,000 jobs that guest workers now fill would continue to exist, but be filled by native Israelis, the national wage bill would increase. Given all of the other challenges that Israel faces in ensuring social cohesiveness, we believe the country would be better off morally, politically, and socially if it would simply bear the cost of phasing out its guest workers.[20]

The fourth option would be to create conditions that would encourage Israeli employers to hire Palestinian commuter workers rather than foreign workers. Obviously, this approach will only be available once the larger Palestinian issues are resolved. In a sense, it is an ideal solution, since it would keep labor costs lower than a complete ban on either Palestinian or guest workers, while at the same time affording many Palestinian workers economic opportunities they might not otherwise have within the borders of their own land. But the time for such an ideal solution may be long in coming.

Compulsory Service

Clearly, the army is one of the central institutions for maintaining social cohesion within Israel. Even without the security threats that require Israel to maintain a strong military establishment, a strong case can be made that the army will have to continue providing some of the social glue—a bare minimum of shared values and experiences—needed to keep Israel's pluralistic society intact.

But the army can perform this social role only so long as *all* Israelis serve *in some capacity*. That is not the case now, nor has it been since the state was established. Many Haredim, and a growing number of others as well, have been exempt from service on religious and other grounds. In addition, for reasons of security and consideration of national sensitivities, Arab citizens are not required to serve in the military.

A critical question that Israelis must resolve in the future is whether both these exemptions should continue. As long as they do, a large number of Israeli citizens will remain outside the mainstream of Israeli society, where informal connections made in the army are often important for one's later life. In addition, the exemptions, especially those granted to men from Haredi Jewish families, breed resentment in many in the rest of the country. This resentment intensifies in times of military crisis, when the call for reserves grows and the danger of casualties magnifies.

We recognize that it may not be politically realistic to require adults of high school graduation age from either the Haredi or the Arab communities to serve in a military capacity. But compulsory service can take other forms. In the case of Haredi Jews, who are now exempt from service, for whom no security issues are present, Israel should seriously consider requiring them to serve in a civilian service corps. This policy could be modeled after the Americorps program in the United States, under which volunteers provide various types of assistance to the disadvantaged or perform other types of community service.[21]

Arabs also could be required to serve in the civilian service—although, because the Arab community understandably would be deeply hostile to a compulsory service requirement, such a move would require proper preparation. Participation in civilian service would have the important collateral benefit of mixing Jews and Arabs and possibly (although not necessarily) of facilitating tolerance within the two groups for each other at some point in the future. Naturally, Arabs could be given the option of carrying out their service in their own communities.

Of course, it is conceivable, if not probable, that the majority of Israelis would view civilian service as second-class or easier service, at least for a while. Nonetheless, by performing at least some service, the Haredi community, in particular, would demonstrate its commitment to the welfare of society overall and, in the process, mute some of the criticism leveled by secular and most religious Jews who now serve in the armed forces that the existing exemptions from service are not warranted. Similarly, service by at least some Arabs in a civilian capacity should erode some of the suspicion, or even hostility, among Israeli Jews toward Arabs (and vice versa).

Political System Reform

The electoral reform adopted in 1992, which separated voting for the Knesset from election of the prime minister, has had a perverse effect: it has strengthened, rather than weakened, the splinter political parties. This trend does not bode well for building cohesion among the various groups in Israeli society. Instead, the likely outcome appears to be the worst of both worlds: on the one hand, continuing stalemate at the top of the Israeli government, which will need to maneuver constantly to maintain a tenuous hold on power by reaching all kinds of side deals with the minority parties; and on the other hand, further fragmentation among Israelis, who increasingly think that they have more in common with their own narrow political parties than with the common welfare of the state as a whole.

We recognize, of course, that coalition building is an essential part of any democracy. Furthermore, even in countries, such as the United States, with two stable, dominant political parties, compromises must take place within each party—and across party lines—in order for government to function. But one thing is clear about stable two-party political systems: they are more likely to unite large segments of the population under one of two roofs than are systems dominated by many parties with increasingly narrow interests.

In March 2001, Israel rescinded the direct election of its prime minister, returning to the previous system, under which citizens voted for a single party. Although this step back is a move in the right direction, it gives undue weight to splinter parties, which frustrates efforts at coalition building, a hallmark of stable pluralistic democracies. As long as the parliamentary system is maintained, it would behoove the country to raise the voting threshold for the seating of parties in the Knesset—now at 1.5 percent of the vote—to some higher level, at least 5 percent. Such a reform not only would be in the narrow political interest of the two dominant parties—Labor and Likud—but also would serve the broader welfare of the entire polity. Changing the threshold is merely an example of reform that deals with the issues technically. Much more than that, public education about the importance of reform is needed.

Would Peace Make a Difference?

Progress toward peace with Palestinians—and, over the longer run, with Syria—would present both opportunities and fundamental challenges to Israeli society and government. On the one hand, peace would enhance the attractiveness of Israel as a magnet for foreign investment, while allowing the nation to reduce even further the fraction of total resources devoted to defense. This, in turn, would allow the Israeli government both to lower taxes and to target greater spending in ways that could help to close the economic gaps between portions of the population and thereby help to ease some of the tensions that are now aggravated by economic disparities.

At the same time, however, peace would force Israelis to confront their own internal challenges in a way they have never been forced to do before. Without a common enemy, would Israel's disparate ethnic and religious groups force the country apart? Or would Israel then—ideally, well before then—summon the courage and political will to bridge its internal divides so that peace does not become its undoing? We cannot pretend to know the answers to these questions.

In the meantime, however, steps are available that would help to narrow the deep and growing differences between Israelis along the various axes discussed here. We have suggested a few of those measures in this chapter. We recognize that most, if not all, are controversial and perhaps politically unrealistic in the short run. But, then again, if Israel does not respond to its divisions in a bold and controversial manner—sooner rather than later—it may find that one or more of its divisions has widened into an unbridgeable chasm and that any pretense of pluralism has disappeared. To avoid that outcome will require active discussion and consideration of approaches that today might be unthinkable, but tomorrow may well be necessary.

CHAPTER SIX

Lessons for Other Countries

W HAT CAN OTHER nations learn from the Israeli experience? Although Israel has much that is unique—especially the security problems it faces both externally and internally—it also has much in common with several other countries (and perhaps many more in the future). For one thing, Israel's per capita income now approaches that of the developed world and, indeed, is on a par with that of a number of European countries, as shown in figure 6-1. Second, Israel has welcomed people from many ethnic backgrounds and, in this respect, is much like certain other developed nations—Australia, Canada, the United States, and, to a lesser extent, the United Kingdom. Third, and perhaps most important, Israel's experiments in pluralism, mainly among its Jewish ethnic groups, and to a lesser extent with regard to Jewish and Arab relations, have been relatively successful, under extraordinary stresses and circumstances. Although we argue in chapter 5 that Israel will need to do even more in the future to keep its internal divisions from significantly weakening the social fabric, we believe there is a presumptive case to be made that Israel's success so far should be examined by other countries that have substantially diverse populations

Figure 6-1. GNP per Capita in Various Countries, 1997

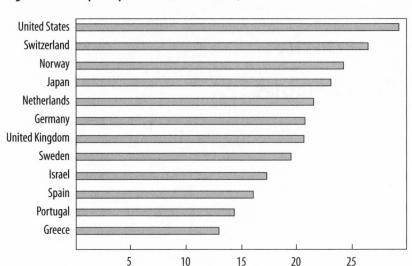

Thousands of U.S. dollars

Source: World Bank, *World Development Report 1999–2000: Entering the Twenty-first Century* (Oxford University Press, 2000).

and are committed to sustaining healthy pluralistic democracies. At the same time, we do not suggest that Israel is a model country that others can and should copy. All we claim is that much can be gained by examining not only Israel's successes but also its failures and mistakes—in both the design and implementation of policy.

We pay special attention in this chapter to what the United States, in particular, may learn both because we know the country well and because the nation not only is open to diversity—indeed, it celebrates that fact—but also will continue to become even more diverse over time. The 2000 census, for example, revealed how much America is changing.[1] One in ten Americans is now foreign born, more than double the fraction three decades ago (although below the nearly 15 percent of the population that was foreign born at the turn of the century). The sources of America's immigrants also have changed dramatically. In the late nineteenth century and through much of the twentieth century, most immigrants came from

Europe; now they come primarily from Latin America, the Caribbean, Asia, and the Middle East.[2] The shift in migration patterns is leading to significant changes in America's racial and ethnic mix. In 1980, 92 percent of the U.S. population identified itself as either non-Hispanic white or black. Twenty years later, in 2000, that number was down to 82 percent, and the Hispanic community roughly equalled the size of the African American community (each at about 12 percent of the population). Twenty-five years from now, non-Hispanic whites likely will account for fewer than two-thirds of American residents, Hispanics will have far surpassed blacks as the nation's largest minority group, and people of Asian descent probably will account for about one in every thirteen American residents. Even this accounting is deceptively homogeneous, since each of the main minority groups is highly diverse itself and each has members with strong ethnic identities and cultures that they would like to preserve.

The United States is not the only developed country with a highly diverse population. As shown in table 6-1, foreign-born residents historically have made up an even larger share of the population in three other industrial countries: Australia, Canada, and Switzerland. Furthermore, in two other European countries—Austria and Germany—the foreign share increased substantially between 1988 and 1998 (the most recent year for which we have data). Even in Japan, where foreigners are relatively rare, their share increased somewhat (from 0.8 to 1.2 percent) during the past ten years due to a modest loosening in 1990 of the country's previously very restrictive immigration policy.

Several factors have contributed to increasing diversity in other so-called rich countries. One is the collective desire for migrants and other low-skilled workers to do jobs that natives prefer not to do—a strong reason why Israel has imported guest workers and, before them, employed large numbers of Palestinians. More recently, the opposite consideration has played an important role: a desire to import highly skilled professionals, especially in information technology, where domestic talent may be limited or more expensive. In addition, in Europe in particular, the collapse of the Berlin Wall unleashed a pent-up demand for immigration to the West among many people in Eastern Europe and Russia.

Looking ahead, we see one other motivation for richer countries other than the United States to accept immigrants—notwithstanding any

Table 6-1. Foreign or Foreign-Born Population in Select OECD Countries, 1988 and 1998

	Number (thousands)		Percent of total population	
Country	1988[a]	1998[b]	1988[a]	1998[b]
Australia[c]	3,753	3,908	22.3	21.1
Austria	344	737	4.5	9.1
Belgium	869	892	8.8	8.7
Canada[c]	4,343	4,971	16.1	17.4
Denmark	142	256	2.8	4.8
Finland	19	85	0.4	1.6
France	3,714	3,597	6.8	6.3
Germany	4,489	7,320	7.3	8.9
Ireland	82	111	2.4	3.0
Italy	645	1,250	1.1	2.1
Japan	941	1,512	0.8	1.2
Netherlands	624	662	4.2	4.4
Norway	136	165	3.2	3.7
Portugal	95	178	1.0	1.8
Spain	360	720	0.9	1.5
Sweden	421	500	5.0	5.6
Switzerland	1,007	1,348	15.2	19.0
United Kingdom	1,821	2,207	3.2	3.8
United States[c]	19,767	26,300	7.9	9.8
Total[d]	43,571	56,719	5.7	6.9

Source: Jonathan Coppel, Jean-Christophe Dumont, and Ignazio Visco, "Trends in Immigration and Economic Consequences," OECD Economics Department Working Paper 284 (Paris: Organization for Economic Cooperation and Development, June 2001), table 2.
a. 1990 for the United States; 1991 for Australia and Canada; 1982 for France.
b. 1990 for France; 1996 for Australia and Canada.
c. Foreign-born population.
d. For those countries shown in the table and, where applicable, for the dates noted in notes a and b.

restrictions that may be imposed in response to the terrorist attack on the United States in September 2001 and its aftermath. Most countries in Western Europe and Japan face the prospect of shrinking native populations in the decades ahead, at the same time as their current residents continue to age. This combination of demographic trends will put increasing pressure on the social insurance systems of these countries, especially those that operate "pay as you go" programs that fund the costs of supporting current retirees out of the wages of the current workforce.[3] A dwindling workforce coupled with a rising dependent population can only mean two things, neither of them politically pleasant: higher social insurance taxes for workers or cuts in benefits for retirees (or both).[4]

Opening the doors to immigrants, even if they are younger than the existing population, cannot or is not likely to remedy the funding problem by itself. According to an Organization for Economic Cooperation and Development study, the net migration required to maintain a constant ratio of retired persons to working adults in Western Europe and Japan already is quite large—in the range of 5 million immigrants a year—and is likely to be in the neighborhood of 20 million annually by 2040.[5] These levels of immigration almost certainly are politically unsustainable, far higher than the roughly 1 million individuals that Western Europe and Japan currently take in each year. But it is likely that even lower annual flows of immigration are not acceptable either. For example, just to prevent a decline in the work force (those between the ages of fifteen and sixty-four), Europe's net immigration would have to nearly quadruple from present levels—to an average of 3.6 million a year. An increase of this magnitude would radically change the face of Europe, such that immigrants and others who are not descendants of present-day Europeans would account for 20–25 percent of Europe's inhabitants by 2050.[6] This level of immigration seems politically unrealistic given the rising anti-immigrant sentiment in much of Western Europe and even in the United Kingdom.[7] At the same time, however, higher levels of immigration are likely to help cover the projected increases in social welfare and retirement costs in Europe in the years ahead.

The economic prospects are even worse for Japan, whose level of immigration is close to zero, but where 700,000 immigrants a year for the next fifty years would be required just to keep the working-age population constant.[8] Understandably, one recent study projects a declining role for Japan in the world economy *unless* it becomes far more open to immigration.[9]

Accordingly, we believe it is likely that both Europe and Japan will decide to accept significantly more immigrants in the future, although precisely how many more we are not prepared to project. Indeed, if recent experience is any guide, some significant number of immigrants may come to Europe—in particular, illegally—whether the countries want them or not. In fact, there are signs of increased immigration already, albeit at varying speeds and in different manners in different countries. A country as insular as France has opened up so much in recent years that Paris has become very much like New York. The creation of the European Union is likely to lead not only to more uniformity in immigration policies across Europe but also to higher levels of immigration.

We do not pretend to know what is the right number and composition of immigrants that Europe, Japan, or even the United States, for that matter, should allow to enter. Ultimately, decisions about levels of immigration come down to value judgments and the kinds of trade-offs between social and economic costs and benefits that each country must make on its own. Nonetheless, we believe that the experience of countries like Israel that have accepted large numbers of different kinds of immigrants can help to inform those decisions. This is because, however many immigrants they accept, nations will face a similar challenge to the one that Israel continues to confront: how to maintain a cohesive, though pluralistic, society.

If others look to Israel, what can or should they find? We close this study by attempting to extract a few answers based on our earlier discussion. But first we take a step back and address the fundamental question of how relevant the Israeli experiment in fact may be. Is not Israel an extreme case, one with extraordinarily deep and unique internal divisions, whose experience, while so far positive, may not be that instructive for other, admittedly diverse, societies? Or, to put it differently, are the stresses that the United States and other developed societies confront likely to be so great that more aggressive actions are called for to maintain social cohesion? Will existing institutions and policies be sufficient to handle any challenge? If not, what is the cost of failing to do so?

The Nature of the Challenge Ahead

On the surface, there appears to be, or will be in the future, as much of a difference in ethnic, national, and racial composition in the United States as there is in Israel. This may be less true of Europe, and certainly of Japan, but nonetheless, if our suppositions are correct, all societies in these regions of the world are becoming more diverse and thus moving in the Israeli direction in this respect.

Take the United States in particular. One of the great triumphs of America so far is that, by and large, the nation's institutions not only tolerate but also encourage separate identities, so long as all Americans continue to share a core commitment to democratic government and to the constitution and laws promulgated under it that allow self-expression and prevent state-sanctioned discrimination on the basis of, among other things, race, religion, and gender. The success is hardly complete, to be sure. Racial division has wracked the country throughout its history and played a central role in the U.S. civil war, an experience that Israel cannot come close to matching. In addition, the United States does a less than perfect job of absorbing its immigrants quickly into society: some suffer or have suffered discrimination (as American blacks have and many still do). Indeed, nativist opposition to immigrants from European countries in the early twentieth century was vigorous, and some vestiges remain with respect to Hispanic and Asian immigrants.

The United States nonetheless has done a relatively good job, so far, in fostering a pluralistic society and forging common bonds among citizens of all backgrounds. Educational and workplace opportunities have played a key role in this effort, as has the immigration process itself, which has consisted of several large-scale, but intermittent, waves of immigrants. Each hiatus (between these waves) has given the society political and social "breathing space" in which to incorporate newcomers. More recently, the media and popular culture, while giving voice to musical and artistic expressions of peoples of different backgrounds, also has allowed each subculture to cross-fertilize so that Americans have managed to share many common values and beliefs. Amitai Etzioni makes this compelling argument in his new book, *The Monochrome Society*.[10]

Drawing on an impressive array of polling evidence, Etzioni demonstrates that Americans of different racial and ethnic backgrounds nonetheless agree on many propositions, among them the notion that high school students need to understand the common history and ideas that bind Americans together and the proposition that public schools need to teach new immigrant children to read, write, and speak English and to be proud to live under America's political system. Further evidence of this cultural blending is a more literal one: an increasing rate of intermarriage between whites and blacks and between Hispanics and whites. To be sure, Etzioni also cites contrary evidence, namely differences between black and white Americans on controversial questions such as affirmative action and other policy issues as well as differences in perceptions of whether "things are getting better or worse" in the public schools. Nonetheless, Etzioni is optimistic, on balance, an outlook he shares with another prominent analyst of American society. According to Roberto Suro, in America, at least so far, ideas generate oneness, and, as long as faith in those ideas remains strong, the country has an extraordinary capacity to absorb people of many nationalities.[11]

Recent political trends strengthen this optimistic view. After a rise in anti-immigrant sentiment in the 1980s and early 1990s—especially in California, through its then-governor Republican Pete Wilson—America has turned much more welcoming toward immigrants. In particular, another Republican, this time a president, George W. Bush, has announced that his administration is considering a policy granting some sort of amnesty to potentially several million illegal Mexican immigrants—an action that would have been politically unthinkable a few years ago, when even the Clinton administration was touting its stringent efforts to control illegal immigration across the U.S.-Mexican border. Also significant is that organized labor, which has been cool and even hostile to new trade agreements, has been very supportive of current and future immigrants—to be sure, out of self-interest, since immigrants represent a large source of potential recruits, but it is a stance that is significant nonetheless.

Another reason for remaining calm in the face of rising diversity is that the political institutions in America—with the country's finely crafted checks and balances among its three branches of government—have, for the most part, been poorly suited to implementing radical change, especially in the absence of an immediate perceived crisis. Indeed, the instances where the United States has taken broad and bold social policy measures—the adoption of the various components of the New Deal in the 1930s or the Marshall Plan and significant upgrading of defense after World War II—reinforce the view that real crisis is necessary to overcome the checks and balances and achieve far-sighted change. The noted economist Mancur Olson provides yet another reason why radical changes are difficult to accomplish in democratic societies: the growth over time in the number and influence of interest groups with offsetting interests, which promotes political gridlock.[12] For these reasons, it has become customary for politicians in the United States to portray any significant change in policy as a response to a crisis—real or manufactured—in order to prod legislators to act and the public to support them in doing so. Recent examples of such attempts, not all of them successful, include the various budget deficit reduction packages of the 1990s (successful); a proposed radical reshaping of the health care system (unsuccessful); the 2001 across-the-board tax cut, like its 1981 predecessor (successful); and, most recently, proposals for a comprehensive energy plan and social security reform by the Bush administration (at this writing, a verdict is still outstanding). The key point, however, is that in America, as in most stable democracies, policy changes tend to be incremental and not particularly forward-looking.

Is there any reason to think differently about the challenges that increasing diversity arising out of increased immigration, among other demographic forces, pose for the years ahead? Several factors or trends suggest that the answer may be an affirmative one. As a threshold matter, it is important to keep in mind that the history of immigration to the United States has not been an effortless process, as more romantic recollections would have it. To the contrary, it has been marked by considerable intergroup competition, conflict, and intolerance. Some degree of conflict can be expected in the future, as the country continues to take in millions of immigrants.

In particular, one troubling trend of the past three decades—interrupted, fortunately, for the last half of the 1990s—has been a rise in income inequality, dating from as early as 1973.[13] While a debate rages among economists as to whether the trend toward greater inequality truly halted in the mid-1990s, it certainly is conceivable that two of the main forces driving the trend before then—increased immigration of people with little formal schooling and therefore low labor market skills, coupled with continued technological change favoring skilled workers—could resume their dominance in the years ahead, without being sufficiently offset by other factors (such as a rising minimum wage, increased unionization, and improvement in the schools). Greater income inequality, in turn, can weaken social glue by increasing frustration among those left behind and eroding social capital—informal networks of associations and public activities—that help to keep societies together. Some evidence has emerged that this has already occurred.[14]

Second, the rising fraction of the population consisting of nonwhite, but also nonblack, immigrants already has contributed to tensions between African Americans, once the dominant minority in America, and members of these other groups. Paradoxically, policies that provide more assistance to immigrants may exacerbate these tensions: although they help to assimilate immigrants, they also create resentment among blacks, who rightly point out that many of them, or their ancestors, did not receive the same kind of help. To the contrary, even after they were freed from slavery, blacks faced continuing discrimination in many facets of life and still do in some.

Third, the sheer scale of the demographic changes that lie ahead—those portending that within five decades white Americans will no longer be the majority of the population—suggests that history could be a poor guide to how American society will cope with its increased diversity in the future. The optimistic view holds that the institutions that now exist, coupled with an apparent rise in tolerance among Americans toward peoples of different races, ethnic origins, and sexual preferences, will be sufficient to maintain social cohesion in the face of these changes. Indeed, since diversity has been a strength of American society so far, contributing to a constantly changing culture and to the ability of Americans to operate well in a global economy, increased diversity in the future may very well further strengthen these advantages. But the risk that cannot be dismissed is that, without more effort by public and private institutions to ensure social cohesion, the increase in diversity on the scale that is envisioned will weaken social bonds, perhaps significantly.

The rapid growth of the Internet also may contribute to a further erosion of common social bonds. One of the great advantages of the Net is that it provides individuals with virtually unlimited access to information from all over the globe. But precisely because it lowers the cost of obtaining information and connecting individuals with others who share their views and beliefs, the Net paradoxically may narrow rather than widen individuals' horizons. More people may choose to obtain information from sources they trust rather than from a commonly watched or read national medium. The number of Americans who obtain their news from the national networks has been dropping steadily, as has readership of some major newspapers. As citizens retreat into their own worlds, they may share less and less with others from different backgrounds. This tendency may help to explain the steep erosion of support for American political institutions—even for American citizenship—reported in surveys among younger Americans.[15]

In sum, it would be a mistake, in our view, for the public and the political leaders to take for granted that even in a country as diverse and politically stable as the United States a healthy respect for pluralism, and an accompanying tolerance for different peoples and points of view, will continue in the face of demographic trends that could pull in the other direction. At the very least, there is a risk that existing institutions and policies—designed to ensure that Americans share a basic commitment to a core set of political values, especially tolerance—may prove insufficient. The same is true, and perhaps even more applicable, to parts of Europe and Japan that have not been as open to immigrants in the past as has the United States but that, for reasons already suggested, may be forced to change in the American (and Israeli) direction in the future.

Of course, whether anticipatory action, in the form of a social insurance policy, should be taken to ensure that a minimum degree of social cohesion exists in a given society depends on the risk that existing institutions will not be up to the task. Perhaps more significant, as a matter of political reality, public institutions in any democratic society tend to change only when they sense a crisis. Thus whether more far-reaching policies *will* be adopted to promote social and political cohesion will depend on the *perception* in any society of the risk of fragmentation.

Why, then, should we look to Israel for lessons about how to address and minimize this risk? We should do so precisely because Israel is an extreme case, having, in our view, confronted challenges to social cohesion—even within the Jewish majority—that are significantly greater than those experienced currently by the United States, Europe, or Japan. Moreover, despite the difficulties that Israel faces in the future—and the need to confront them in ways outlined in chapter 5—Israel has been largely successful in keeping its society together under very difficult circumstances. Those successes, and the policies and the institutions that produced them, at the very least can serve as potential models for other countries, like the United States, Europe, and Japan, that may face growing challenges to maintaining social cohesion in the future as they, too, admit more immigrants and thus experience greater diversity within their populations.

To be sure, the institutions and policies we survey in this chapter are more radical than those generally in place outside Israel. For this reason, we are under no illusions that any of our suggestions will be politically feasible, or even socially necessary, anytime soon, if ever. Nonetheless, just as many companies and organizations encourage their managers and workers to think "outside the box" to come up with creative approaches to addressing new challenges and creating new products and services, we believe it can be useful for thoughtful leaders and the public to do likewise, if for no other reason than to put policy suggestions "on the shelf," where they might be located if and when the circumstances are more amenable to significant change. In that spirit, we offer the following broad ideas, drawn from the Israeli experience.

Immigrant Absorption

If one lesson stands out from Israeli immigration policy, it is this: nations that truly want more immigrants but are worried about their socioeconomic ability to absorb them can minimize potential tensions by adopting comprehensive immigrant absorption programs. Recall from earlier chapters that, on their arrival in Israel, immigrants are given language training, housing and job search assistance, and economic support in their first few months in their new land. This effort extends well beyond what other developed nations do for their immigrants, which is to leave them to their own devices or to the assistance of family members already living in the country. In essence, these countries follow a "sink or swim" approach to immigrant absorption. Why the difference?

One obvious reason is that, except for guest workers, Israel's immigrants automatically become citizens, whereas, in other developed countries, immigrants first are accepted provisionally for some period of time (most often in order to work) and then must apply separately for citizenship, which typically requires the individual to pass some kind of test. Knowing at the outset that its immigrants will become citizens gives the state (Israel, for purposes of this book) greater incentives to integrate individuals and their families into the cultural milieu and language of the country. Where immigrants must wait for some period in order to qualify for citizenship, countries have no assurance that all the monies they spend on absorption programs—language training, housing assistance, and the like—will actually support future citizens.

Second, to the extent that other developed nations have accepted immigrants on the basis of family reunification more than level of skills—essentially the long-standing policy in the United States—the tendency is to place the burden of absorption on family members already in the country.[16] Furthermore, in the United States in particular, this policy has meant that large numbers of immigrants have been admitted with skills that are well below those of the population as a whole. While this ensures a large pool of unskilled labor for employers and wealthier families who otherwise would have to pay higher wages to natives to get the same jobs done, many low-skilled native workers with whom they compete resent the influx of immigrants, which contributes to ethnic and racial tensions (and in parts of Europe, where unemployment has been much higher than in the United States, to acts of hatred and violence directed toward immigrants).

This explains a third reason why Western nations have not adopted more comprehensive immigration absorption policies: doing so would expose their governments to the charge that they are unfairly favoring new arrivals at the expense of helping natives to improve their living standards. In fact, some native Israelis have raised precisely this charge with respect to the substantial assistance given to immigrants from the former Soviet Union.[17] Fortunately for the stability of Israeli society, most Jewish residents do not harbor resentment because they share a common feeling of responsibility for refugees of at least the same nominal faith or identity (Judaism). Israel, therefore, has found it politically easier to maintain a comprehensive immigrant absorption policy than other countries that also take in substantial numbers of immigrants.

Although these reasons explain past differences in absorption policies between many developed economies and Israel, societies that continue to take in more immigrants may want to consider moving in Israel's

direction—in other words, toward more comprehensive absorption policies. At a minimum, more effort could be given to ensuring that immigrants learn the native language. A more far-reaching effort would subsidize
the completion of at least a high school education for those who do not
have that level of schooling—most practically by supporting programs
that workers can attend at night to upgrade their skills. Such assistance
also should be available to natives who may be in the work force but want
to return to school.

Still, even a comprehensive absorption policy cannot eliminate all frictions, as our description of the schisms in Israeli society well attests. But
think for a moment how deep those divisions would be if Israel had not
gone to such great lengths to extend a welcoming hand to its immigrants
and to assist them so greatly in adapting to their new country. It is not clear
whether Israeli society could have survived, or if it did, whether it could
have achieved such impressive economic gains and instilled such allegiance
to its country (and to its armed forces). By similar reasoning, the "absorp-
tive capacity" of other countries in accepting immigrants—by which we
mean the ability to maintain a functioning pluralistic society—should depend heavily on the extent of their efforts to welcome and integrate immigrants. The more effort that is expended on promoting integration, the
more immigrants a nation should be able to accommodate.

An alternative approach, of course, is to change the composition of
immigrants so that only those with strong skills to begin with are admitted to the country. Highly educated individuals, especially professionals in
the fields of medicine and information technology, tend to have relatively
little difficulty integrating into new societies and finding employment because their skills, areas of employment, and training are in demand everywhere. They assimilate into their new countries through the new colleagues
they meet and work with at their new jobs as much as through family
connections. Moreover, because they tend to take jobs in sectors with a
strong demand for labor, highly trained immigrants often do not displace
natives, or, if they do, the effect is not transparent and thus generates little
resentment. In contrast, immigrants with few skills directly compete with
less-skilled natives, for whom there is often insufficient demand. Indeed,
that is why George Borjas of Harvard, a prominent researcher, finds that
immigration has suppressed the wages of blue-collar and less-skilled work-

ers in a number of developed economies. For these reasons, countries such as Australia and Canada have emphasized skill above family connections in choosing to which immigrants to permit entry.

But not all developed nations can pursue a skills-centered immigration policy without running substantial risk of being accused by developing countries of promoting a "brain drain." As economists might put it, there is a "tragedy of the commons" aspect to attempts by all developed (and perhaps even some developing) economies seeking to "skim the cream" of the talent in developing countries. Although some successful immigrants in richer countries start businesses that employ individuals from their home countries—Indian, Chinese, and Israeli entrepreneurs in the United States are excellent examples—this tendency is not universal.[18] As a result, it is not clear for many countries whether a tolerant attitude toward the emigration of their "best and brightest" is in their national interest, especially when taking into account the importance of higher education as a key to economic growth. If countries do their best to educate their most talented citizens, only to find the best of them leaving and never returning, the "leakage" of human capital, while potentially beneficial in the long run, can diminish the short-run incentives to upgrade education generally.

Moreover, strong countervailing political pressures from families of existing immigrants within destination countries can prevent heavier reliance on skills-based immigration policies, and this pressure acts to brake any shift in immigration policy toward one that puts skills ahead of family reunification. This helps to explain why the United States, in particular, has continued to maintain its current immigration policy. Countries that put more emphasis on family reunification than on skills thus squarely face the same challenge that Israel has had to confront: finding ways to acculturate new arrivals into the society so that they share the prevailing political values of the population and, at the same time, are able to find suitable and productive employment.

Systematic Language Instruction

The Israeli policy of providing new arrivals with systematic language training *before* they are expected to take a job has been a powerful melding force that has helped to preserve social cohesion. By analogy, therefore, other countries could provide similar language acquisition programs for immigrants seeking work permits as a preliminary stage in seeking citizenship. In fact, certain countries—notably Sweden and the Netherlands—have provided extensive language training to their immigrants.

We recognize, however, that, at least in the United States (if not in other countries), it would not be feasible to prevent immigrants who lack facility in English from accepting employment because many would work informally. But this should not rule out the use of greater incentives on the part of both the federal and state governments for immigrants to learn English and to upgrade their education.

Language instruction should not be viewed as a punishment, but instead as a necessary tool to function in a new society. The United States, where bilingual education was much the rage for a while, seems to be coming around to this view, at least at the state level. In the late 1990s California adopted a voter-initiated proposition (Proposition 227) that ended bilingual education in elementary through high school. Test score evidence since 1998, when the proposition became effective, indicates that the students from families whose native tongue is not English have improved their school performance markedly.[19] Other states are considering initiatives similar to California's. For a nation that is becoming ever more diverse, teaching all students in English would appear to be critical to ensuring that all adult citizens in the United States have at least a minimum of shared experience and knowledge. Moreover, because being able to speak and write English is essential for all but low-skilled jobs, doing more to facilitate the English skills of immigrants would help to improve their living standards.[20]

In chapter 5, we suggest that Israel could improve social cohesion among its Arab and Jewish citizens by promoting bilingual familiarity, although not necessarily through bilingual *education*. That is, we do not suggest that the current policy of having Arab and Jewish schools teach students primarily in their own language be abandoned, but rather that it be supplemented with greater language familiarity. This is where the differences between the United States and Israel matter. Fortunately, the history of hostility between various hyphenated Americans and other Americans is not nearly as deep as it is between Arabs and Jews. For this reason, we accept the reality that Arab children will continue to be taught primarily in Arabic, while Jewish children will be taught primarily in Hebrew. Ideally, this would not be the case: since Hebrew is the dominant language of Israel and will remain so, it would be better for all children to learn solely in Hebrew. In the United States, this compromise with reality is not necessary, nor does it serve the interest of the children of any minority. All students should be taught in English, the language of the country.

Immigrants seeking citizenship should display more than just a facility with the home-country language, of course. They must understand the country's social mores, history, and government. Nations generally require applicants for citizenship to pass a rudimentary test of such knowledge, but here too, more could be offered in the way of instruction. If nations want their new arrivals to become better integrated with their societies, they must give them a core base of knowledge with which to do that. In the United States, immigrants are left to acquire such information on their own, and there is little government support for teaching it, except for the *children* of illegal immigrants, who are entitled to attend primary and secondary school, but not to attend college without a student or work visa. Using the same model that we urge for language instruction, we suggest that government provide, either directly or indirectly, all adult immigrants seeking citizenship with the rough equivalent of a high school civics course. This bare minimum in education merits serious consideration, in our view, regardless of whether the government decides to subsidize the completion of a full high school curriculum (as we suggest).

In the United States, children of illegal immigrants face another problem: If they succeed in being accepted to college, they typically must pay higher foreign tuition and are not eligible for financial assistance, which effectively makes it impossible for many, if not most, to attend.[21] It is hard to justify spending upward of $60,000 to educate such children through high school and shutting the door on them thereafter. As a purely economic matter, such a policy wastes human capital: who knows how many of these potential college students would otherwise make meaningful contributions to our society? The policy often results in personal tragedy for students whose hopes for advancement in American society are dashed by their inability to attend college.

A more rational policy would be to bar colleges from charging lawful graduates of American high schools, even if their parents are living in this country illegally, the tuition it assesses foreign students (without necessarily requiring colleges to offer financial assistance). To be sure, such a policy, at the margin, would provide incentives for even more illegal immigration than now occurs. We suspect, although we cannot prove, that this effect would not be significant. One way to find out would be to try the policy for a limited period and see how much additional pressure it places on border patrols that now attempt to keep out illegal immigrants.

Compulsory Service

Another potentially important lesson Israel can teach other countries is the virtue of a mandatory service requirement for all residents, at some early point in life, such as immediately after high school graduation. This is already policy in some other developed countries, such as Switzerland and Germany, which require their male high school graduates to serve at least some time in the military.[22]

Beyond the obvious security objective, compulsory service has several related social benefits. It would bring together individuals from all walks of life and different socioeconomic, ethnic, and racial backgrounds during their formative years and put them in a common environment where they have no other choice than to get along with each other. An editorial in the *Wall Street Journal* (of all places) observed in 1981 that mandatory service in the American context would constitute "a means for acculturation, acquainting young people with their fellow Americans of all different races, creeds, and economic backgrounds."[23] Another important function of compulsory service is to instill in all who serve a sense of obligation to the entire society, a lesson that is learned not only during the service itself but also throughout an individual's life.

To be sure, there are many objections to a *military* service requirement. For some, any mandate at all entails an unwarranted, if temporary, loss of freedom for the individuals involved and, for those put in harm's way in the armed forces, potentially a loss of life. Others no doubt will point to the unique security problems that Israel confronts and thus its need for a draft. In other countries, such as the United States, where there are no such immediate security threats, the case for compulsory military service looks much weaker.

We are not suggesting that compulsory service automatically means *military* service. As we outline in chapter 5, service can take the form of community service (assisting the disadvantaged, serving as a teacher's aide, and the like) in a much-expanded version of the Americorps program, as Senator John McCain has suggested. In the United States, some very limited movement already has occurred in this direction. High schools in many communities now require all students to perform a minimum number of hours of "community service" during their three or four years in high school (a requirement unheard of when the American author of this volume was in high school). The universal service requirement we are suggesting would be considerably longer, on the order of a year, and would be carried out in a group setting. In addition, those serving in the civilian program would live away from home, in a dormitory setting, much like those who now serve in the military. Moreover, unlike many current community service programs in which students from moderate- and higher-income families satisfy the requirement by assisting programs that deliver services to local residents, who often may be of the same socioeconomic status as the students themselves, the program we have in mind would aim to deliver benefits to more disadvantaged populations.

For many individuals, their year in compulsory service may be the only time in their lives when they mix for substantial periods of time, and on an equal footing, with persons who come from very different backgrounds. Although civilian service may not be as intense as service in the armed forces, if implemented in a group setting, it nonetheless could help individuals to develop a deeper understanding of and appreciation for others at a time in their lives—just after graduation from high school (or college or graduate school)—when their adult personalities are forming and their future career choices may be made.[24]

Indeed, the relative lack of diversity in many American public schools strengthens the case for a compulsory service requirement. Inner-city public schools in many large metropolitan areas are populated predominantly by African American and other minority students, while their suburban counterparts are attended by students from upper-middle-class, often white, families. Meanwhile, even in colleges where student bodies are made up of students from many different backgrounds, this diversity may not be true of *individual classes*. In any event, the college environment generally does not lend itself to cooperative endeavors by students, as the year of service could be structured to ensure, but instead rewards individual performance and thus is often highly competitive.

The movement toward greater choice in primary and secondary schools, whether accomplished through charter schools, vouchers, or tax credits, also somewhat ironically helps to strengthen the case for a mandatory service requirement after high school. Although choice may well provide an important market-based device for improving school and student performance, it necessarily enhances the power of self-selection by parents and their children. One predictable result is that many more students could sort themselves into schools with student populations of similar background (this should not be true of students from the inner city, but could well be the case for students in suburban areas). To the extent this occurs, students in the future may be even less exposed than they are now to persons from a different background. Compulsory service after high school would help to offset this effect.

At the same time, the mandatory feature of service admittedly would have strong opponents. In the past, many have advanced arguments ranging from the large potential for make-work that such a requirement could entail to the libertarian objection that it deprives individuals of their freedom. Organized labor may object to the extent that those serving in the program perform functions that are now undertaken by paid workers. Furthermore, any service would have short-run costs. One rough estimate of gross government cost in the United States would be on the order of $25 billion annually (roughly 2.5 million high school graduates a year times $10,000 in annual support costs)—a substantial sum. In addition, individuals would incur economic costs as well because they would delay by one year their entry into either college or the labor force, which would reduce (modestly) their lifetime incomes.

For these reasons, a more politically attractive alternative to mandatory service is an expanded *voluntary* service program. For example, one could envision additional incentives for young people to serve in a civilian capacity: assistance with college or, for those with college or graduate degrees, loan forgiveness. A voluntary program almost certainly would be less costly than a mandatory program. But because, by design, a voluntary program would attract only those most interested in serving, it would not be as effective in promoting the cross-fertilization of individuals from different backgrounds as would a mandatory program.

Faith-Based Delivery of Social Services

Other countries also can learn from the positives and negatives of the Israeli experience in delivering social services through nongovernmental, especially religious, institutions. This is particularly relevant in the United States, where the Bush administration in early 2001 launched its "faith-based" social service initiative, a broad policy aimed at removing legal barriers to religious organizations receiving government aid for promoting social welfare—providing remedial education, drug rehabilitation, and the like. Although the new policy has attracted support from both major political parties, it also has generated its share of criticism from both. The main concern is the fear that it will compromise the constitutional prohibition on mixing religion and the state.

Israel has had the equivalent of the Bush policy—actually one that goes even further—for some time and potentially provides some useful lessons for other countries in this regard. At one time, Israel's largest nongovernmental social service organization was the Histadrut, which provided education, health care, retirement support, and housing, among other services, to its members.[25] Today, Shas (the Sephardi-Haredi party) stands out as an active nongovernmental organization performing religious and social service functions primarily in education, as described in chapter 3. Nongovernmental organizations also play a role in the Arab sector. Somewhat like Shas, the Islamic Movement and its organization plays an influential role in the religious, social, social service, educational, and political realms of Arab Israeli society. Both Shas in the Jewish sector and the Islamic Movement in the Arab sector use their systems and organizations to advance their partisan political agendas, to no less an extent (and at times a greater extent) than their social goals.

There is a reasonably strong consensus in Israeli society that the delivery of social services through nongovernmental organizations is a good thing and may be a more effective way of delivering those services than the government.[26] Moreover, to the extent that they are funded from private parties, these organizations can—and do—add to the overall level of resources aimed at social services. Yet mixing social service delivery with political operations has its drawbacks. The Israeli experience demonstrates how nongovernmental organizations can use their control over the delivery of services to recruit and maintain membership and political support. Indeed, religious institutions in both the Arab and Jewish sectors used to avoid relations with municipal or central government authorities and, largely in an effort to build and maintain their own constituencies, delivered their services separately. Israel's experience indicates that, however well intentioned, relying on nongovernmental institutions, especially those that are centered around religious institutions, may contribute to the fragmentation of society, especially if the groups with which they are identified or affiliated fail to show tolerance for members of other groups with whom they may not agree. This outcome should be weighed against the possibility, or even likelihood, that alternative delivery systems "work better"—that is, produce better outcomes at the same or even lower cost than government-administered social programs.

Israel's experience in mixing religion and state provides another important lesson for other countries, although not one that many Israeli residents would wish to recognize. As we discuss in chapter 2, Israel has never had a constitution, and its very creation, as a homeland for Jews from around the world, explains why it has no history of separating church and state, as is the case in the United States, for example. If the majority of Israelis were religious Jews who accepted the legitimacy of Orthodox Jewish pronouncements on areas of civil law such as marriage, citizenship, and the like, then the deference of the state to religious law in these areas, as well as the other ways in which the government defers to the Haredi community, would not create as much tension as now exists between secular and religious Jews. But precisely because most Israelis are secular, the close mixing of religion and state has been a source of growing division among Israelis. Looking at this outcome, Americans should be gratified with their constitutional separation between church and state, which however controversial it still may be, at least reduces the potential for the kind of conflicts that are present in Israeli society (although religion still accounts for divisions within American society as well).[27]

Concluding Remarks

Israel is not alone in facing the social consequences—challenges and opportunities—of a highly diverse population. Other countries around the world, especially developed societies, are confronting the same issues. A central objective common to all of these countries is to ensure that all citizens share a sufficiently common core base of values, knowledge, and tolerance that the overall society remains stable, while fostering improvements in living standards and a sense of community throughout the population.

It has been evident for some time that countries make a mistake if they believe that they can do much more than achieve pluralism. The melting pot may remain an ideal in some quarters, but in societies that are growing increasingly heterogeneous in religion, ethnic background, and race, it is impossible to expect to melt away all differences between people. Nor would it be wise. Societies flourish because of differences among their people—just as trade and commerce would not exist between peoples and nations if not for differences in comparative talents, resources, and levels of expertise. Our modest hope is that, by looking at the experiences of one nation that is attempting to accommodate and nurture these differences, other nations can profit as they chart their own course for the future.

Notes

Chapter One

1. Our reference here regards Judaism as a national identity more than a religion. As we discuss later, the majority of Jews in Israel do not define themselves as "religious" in the same sense of the term as many readers do.

2. From the very beginning, Israel has formally extended full social and political rights to all its citizens regardless of religion. In particular, Israel's Declaration of Independence (*Megilat Ha'atzmaut*) refers to the country as a "Jewish state in *Eretz Yisroel* (the Land of Israel) . . . which will guarantee complete equality of social and political rights without regard to religion, race, or sex." Many Arabs and others question, however, whether Israeli society lives up to these ideals in practice.

3. The male plural of Hebrew nouns tends to end in "im." That is why we typically refer to Sephardim or Haredim, for example, rather than use the English plural, Sephardis or Haredis.

4. Ashkenazim are those with origins in North America or Europe, and Sephardim are those with origins in Arabic-speaking Islamic countries in North Africa and the Middle East. Neither of these terms properly describes their origin, and there are many differences within them. However, both are commonly used among the Israeli public, and thus, for simplicity's sake, we use these two somewhat inaccurate terms throughout the book.

5. Outside Israel, the Haredi community is commonly referred to as Ultra-Orthodox, a term that distinguishes Haredim from other religious groups but does not truly describe their uniqueness. Accordingly, we use the Hebrew term Haredi throughout the book.

Chapter Two

1. See Yaakov Kop, "Population Groups and Trends: Demographic Effects," in Yaakov Kop, ed., *Israel's Social Services 1998* (Jerusalem: Center for Social Policy Studies, 1998).

2. See Moshe Lissak, "The New Immigrants from the Former Soviet Union: Segregation versus Integration," in Yaakov Kop, ed., *Israel's Social Services 1994–95* (Jerusalem: Center for Social Policy Studies, 1996).

3. Moshe Lissak, "Major Schisms in Israel Society," in Yaakov Kop, ed., *Pluralism in Israel: From Melting Pot to Salad Bowl* (Jerusalem: Center for Social Policy Studies, 2000).

4. See Aharon Cohen, *Israel and the Arab World* (Funk and Wagnalls, 1970).

5. See Oren Yiftachel, "The Political Geography of Ethnic Protest: Nationalism, Deprivation, and Regionalism among Arabs in Israel," *Transactions of the Institute of British Geographers*, vol. 22, no. 1 (1997): 91–110.

6. See Cohen, *Israel and the Arab World*.

7. The Israeli Arab support for Maki may have to do with the fact that the Soviet bloc became systematically anti-Israeli. With the rise of other Arab militant national parties in later years, Maki (later Rakah) lost much of its support to pure Arab nationalist parties.

8. Noah Lewin-Epstein, Majid Al-Haj, and Moshe Semyonov, *The Arabs in Israel in the Labor Market* (Jerusalem: Floersheimer Institute for Policy Studies, 1994).

9. Lewin-Epstein, Al-Haj, and Semyonov, *Arabs in Israel in the Labor Market*.

10. Population figures are for 1997.

11. The notion that Sharon's visit "triggered" the uprising is hotly contested both within and outside Israel, in light of statements by Palestinians that the uprising was preorganized and that the Sharon visit (before his election as prime minister) provided a convenient excuse for its initiation.

12. See Kop, "Population Groups and Trends."

13. See Rita Sever, "Anatomy of Immigration, *Aliya,* and Immigrant Absorption in Israel," in Yaakov Kop, ed., *Pluralism in Israel: From Melting Pot to Salad Bowl* (Jerusalem: Center for Social Policy Studies, 2000).

14. Ministry of Immigrant Absorption, *Annual Report* (Jerusalem: Ministry of Immigrant Absorption, 1998).

15. The assistance program given to immigrants does not apply to foreign workers. These workers are not immigrants but rather reside and work in Israel on temporary resident or "long-term tourist" visas.

16. See Itzhak Schnell, *Policy toward Foreign Workers in Israel* (Jerusalem: Center for Social Policy Studies, 2001).

17. This policy was originally set by the British Mandate, which held that these areas of personal status would be the province of each major religion. Thus Christian and Moslem marriage, divorce, and burial are handled by their respective religious establishments, according to their specific denominations. In recent years, the religious monopoly over burial has begun to crack as court decisions have led to the establishment of secular cemeteries.

18. Many secular Israelis, however, still observe some of the key Jewish holidays: Rosh Hoshannah (the Jewish New Year), Yom Kippur (the day of repentance), Succoth (a major fall holiday), and Passover (which marks the deliverance of the Jews from slavery in Egypt roughly 4,000 years ago). See Shlomit Levy, Hanna Levinsohn, and Elihu Katz, *Beliefs, Observances, and Social Interaction among Israeli Jews* (Jerusalem: Louis Guttman Israel Institute of Applied Social Research, 1993).

19. Yosseph Shilhav uses the number of special male gas masks distributed during the Gulf War to estimate the number of Ultra-Orthodox Jews. These special full-face gas masks were distributed to men who would not shave their beards (in accordance with Ultra-Orthodox beliefs) to fit the regular gas masks. About 100,000 of these masks were requested, which represents about 8 percent of all the gas masks distributed during the Gulf War. See Yosseph Shilhav, "The Emergence of Ultra-Orthodox Neighborhoods in Israeli Urban Centers," in Efraim Ben-Zadok, ed., *Local Communities and the Israeli Polity* (State University of New York Press, 1993), pp. 57–183.

20. Shilhav, "The Emergence of Ultra-Orthodox Neighborhoods."

21. There is not a one-to-one correlation between voting behavior and being either religious or secular. In other words, there is a distinction between voting for religious parties and being religious. Indeed, many religious voters do vote for secular parties.

22. Haredi youth gain exemption from their army service by studying at a registered *yeshiva* (full-time religious learning center) for the equivalent of the duration of their army service.

23. An example of the courts' intervention was the forcing of municipal religious councils to include female and non-Orthodox representatives.

24. See Sever, "Anatomy of Immigration, *Aliya,* and Immigrant Absorption."

25. Israel's intention was to create a law that would enable and benefit all Jews (defined in the widest way). In order to do so, the critieria set in the law used a countermirror of the Nuremberg laws, in which the Nazis defined someone as Jewish if one of the grandparents was Jewish.

26. Ironically, emotions run highest on this issue *outside* Israel, principally in the United States, the home of the largest number of Jews in the disapora and a source of strong support for the state of Israel. In the United States, many

in the non-Orthodox majority resent the fact that the state of Israel does not recognize conversion or marriages that are conducted in Israel by Conservative or Reform rabbis (who act according to the doctrines prevailing among American non-Orthodox Jews). Within Israel, the limitation is not of great relevance, as only a small number of religious observants belong to the Conservative or Reform movements. Unfortunately, secular Israelis do not give much thought to the issue.

27. There is, however, an intensified trend of intermarriage between both groups, as discussed in greater detail later in this chapter. See Yechezkel Dar, Nura Resh, and Rachel Erhard, "Perceiving Social Cleavages and Inequalities: The Case of Israeli Adolescents," *Youth and Society,* vol. 30, no. 1 (1989): 32–58. Recent research indicates a rising rate of intermarriage across ethnic lines. See Kop, "Population Groups and Trends"; Yossi Shavit and Chaya Stier, "Ethnic and Educational Assortative Mating: Changing Marriage Patterns in Israel," *Megamot,* no. 2 (1997): 207–25.

28. Yossi Yonah, "Cultural Pluralism and Education: The Israeli Case," *Interchange,* vol. 4, no. 25 (1994): 349–65.

29. Lev Luis Grinberg, *Public Activists of Histadrut and Local Authorities— The Ethnic Dimension,* Research 33 (Jerusalem: Institute for Israel Studies, 1989). For another interpretation of this trend, see Yonah, "Cultural Pluralism and Education."

30. Meanwhile, the Ashkenazi-Sephardi schism has become less problematic than it was in the past. The improvement can be attributed to the rise in the general standard of living of the Sephardi population, coupled with the rise in the number of Sephardim holding important state positions. At present, the president, defense minister, and the Israeli army's chief of staff are all Sephardim.

31. Without delving into the details, it should be noted that there are significant differences between Ashkenazi and Sephardi Haredim.

32. Eliezer Don-Yechiya, "Religion and Ethnicity in Israeli Politics: The Religious Parties and the Elections to the Twelfth Knesset," *State, Government, and International Relations,* vol. 32 (1990): 11–54.

33. Emanuel Gutmann, "The Religious Cleavage," in Moshe Lissak and Baruch Knei-Paz, eds., *Israel towards the Year 2000: Society, Politics, and Culture* (Jerusalem: Magness Press, 1996), pp. 61–73; Neri Horowitz, "The 'Chared Leumi' and the 'Chardalnik,' New Types in Israeli Politics," *Mifne,* no. 14 (1996): 25–30; Michael Shashar, "Israel and the Territories: Religious Attitudes," *Judaism,* vol. 36, no. 4 (1987): 433–42.

34. Amiram Gonen and Rassem Khamaisi, *Trends in the Geographical Distribution of the Arab Population of Israel* (Jerusalem: Floersheimer Institute for Policy Studies, 1993); Yoram Bar-Gal, "Arab Penetration and Settlement in Nazreth Illit," in Arnon Soffer, ed., *Residential and Internal Migration Patterns among the*

Arabs of Israel (University of Haifa, Jewish Arab Center, 1986), pp. 51–64; Ghazi Falah, "Living Together Apart: Residential Segregation in Mixed Arab-Jewish Cities in Israel," *Urban Studies,* vol. 33, no. 6 (1996): 823–57; Akiva Deutsch, "Social Contacts and Social Relationships between Jews and Arabs Living in a Mixed Neighborhood in an Israeli Town," in Akiva Deutsch and Gitta Tulea, eds., *Social and Cultural Integration in Israel* (Ramat-Gan: Bar-Ilan University, Sociological Institute for Community Studies, 1988), pp. 65–93; Shilhav, *The Emergence of Haredi Neighborhoods.*

35. Shlomo Hasson and Amiram Gonen, *The Cultural Tension within Jerusalem's Jewish Population* (Jerusalem: Floersheimer Institute for Policy Studies, 1997); Sara Hershkovitz, "Residential Segregation by Religion: A Conceptual Framework," *Tijdschrift Voor Economische en Sociale Geografie,* vol. 78, no. 1 (1987): 44–52. The segregation in housing patterns in these areas is not a product of planned social policy, but largely the result of individual policy preferences.

36. Joel Greenberg, "A Land of Tribes, Again," *New York Times,* May 9, 1999.

37. Raymond Jubrin, "Characteristics of the Arab Population in Israel," *Economy and Labour,* vol. 9 (1994): 213–34; Aluf Hareven, "Equality and Integration," *Sikkuy's Report 1994–1995* (Jerusalem: Sikkuy Association for the Advancement of Equal Opportunity, 1995); Lewin-Epstein, Al-Haj, and Semyonov, *Arabs in Israel in the Labor Market.*

38. Israeli authorities have also wanted to avoid putting Israeli Arabs in situations in which they may have to fight against their "brethren" in case of war between Arab countries and Israel.

39. Council of Economic Advisers, *Economic Report of the President, 2000* (Government Printing Office, 2000).

40. See Richard D. Alba, "Assimilation's Quiet Tide," *Public Interest,* vol. 119 (Spring 1995): 3–18.

41. See Roderick Harrison and Claudette Bennett, "Racial and Ethnic Diversity," in Reynolds Farley, ed., *State of the Union: America in the 1990s,* vol. 2 (New York: Russell Sage Foundation, 1995), pp. 141–210.

42. See Rochelle Stanfield, "Blending of America," *National Journal,* September 13, 1997.

43. One advantage, though, in contrast with the U.S. system, is that one cannot ascend to office without majority support. This happened most recently in the United States, where President Bush was elected despite receiving only a minority of the popular vote.

44. The presence of Ralph Nader in the 2000 presidential race is widely regarded as having cost then–vice president Gore the election, and many analysts believe that Ross Perot may have cost then-president Bush reelection in 1992.

Chapter Three

1. Central Bureau of Statistics, *Statistical Abstract of Israel*, vol. 48 (Jerusalem: Central Bureau of Statistics, 1997), p. 1-55.

2. The influx of immigrants was associated with other demographic changes, notably an increase in the number and share of the elderly, a rise in the number of smaller households (including many composed of single parents or individuals), and an increase in education-intensive occupations.

3. Central Bureau of Statistics, *Statistical Abstract of Israel*, vol. 51 (Jerusalem: Central Bureau of Statistics, 2000), p. 3-5.

4. Central Bureau of Statistics, *Statistical Abstract of Israel*, vol. 51, p. 3-23.

5. Central Bureau of Statistics, *Statistical Abstract of Israel*, vol. 51, p. 3-23.

6. When speaking of "Arabs," we sometimes refer to statistics that count individuals who classify themselves as Muslim, which is the dominant subgroup within the Arab sector.

7. In the past, another consideration in deciding the number of children was the probability of survival. When infant and child mortality was high, people used to give birth to a larger number of children than desired so as to offset the risk of early mortality and yield the desired family size. This consideration has lost its importance as infant mortality has declined so dramatically.

8. See Dan Eshbal and Arnon Sofer, "The Palestinian Refugees since 1948: Background and Alternatives," *Journal of National Defense Studies* (National Defense College, Israeli Defense Forces), vol. 1 (June 2001).

9. After the 1967 war, Israel annexed East Jerusalem, which it had captured from the Jordanians.

10. Central Bureau of Statistics, *Statistical Abstract of Israel*, vol. 51, p. 2-57.

11. Central Bureau of Statistics, *Statistical Abstract of Israel*, vol. 51, p. 2-48.

12. Central Bureau of Statistics, *Statistical Abstract of Israel*, vol. 48, p. 9-6.

13. Central Bureau of Statistics, *Statistical Abstract of Israel*, vol. 48, p. 3-13.

14. Central Bureau of Statistics, *Statistical Abstract of Israel*, vol. 48, p. 3-22.

15. Central Bureau of Statistics, *Statistical Abstract of Israel*, vol. 48, p. 3-17.

16. Central Bureau of Statistics, *Statistical Abstract of Israel*, vol. 48, p. 2-86.

17. Because the official statistics speak of continents of origin only up to the second generation, the grandchildren of immigrants from various continents are defined as being of Israeli origin.

18. Central Bureau of Statistics, *Statistical Abstract of Israel*, vol. 48, p. 2-85.

19. Population projections are known to be a very delicate business. Just as an example, in 1985 the Central Bureau of Statistics published a forecast of Israel's population for the year 2000 in two alternatives. It predicted a total population of 5.3 million to 5.5 million. The actual figure was 6.3 million. The corresponding prediction for the Jewish population was between 4.1 million and 4.3 million. The actual figure was 5.1 million. The main cause for this significant disparity is

that no demographer could have predicted the mass immigration from Russia, just as very few predicted the fall of the Soviet empire in 1989–90.

Chapter Four

1. Majid Al-Haj, *Education, Empowerment, and Control: The Case of the Arabs in Israel* (State University of New York Press, 1995); Oren Yiftachel, "Research on Jewish-Arab Relations in Israel: Public Policy, Social Gaps, and Political Influences," *State, Government, and International Relations 1995*, vol. 40 (1995): 185–224.

2. Azmi Bishara, "The Arab in Israel: A Study in a Split Political Debate," in Pinhas Ginossar and Bareli Ave, eds., *Zionism: A Contemporary Controversy* (Sede Boqer: Ben-Gurion University of the Negev, Ben-Gurion Research Center, 1996), pp. 312–39; Aluf Hareven, "The Possibilities of a Common Civil Society for Jews and Arabs in Israel," in Yaakov Landau, Issad Ganam, and Aluf Hareven, eds., *Israel's Arab Citizens at the Turn of the Twenty-First Century* (Jerusalem: Magnus Press, 1995); Ra'anan Cohen, *Complicated Loyalty: Society and Politics in the Arab Sector* (Tel Aviv: Am Oved, 1990); Yitzhak Rater, "Between a 'Jewish State' and a 'State for Its Residents': The Position of the Arabs in Israel in the Era of Peace," in Yaakov Landau, Issad Ganam, and Aluf Hareven, eds., *Israel's Arab Citizens at the Turn of the Twenty-First Century* (Jerusalem: Magnus Press, 1995); Nadim Rouhana, *The Arabs in Israel: Psychological, Political, and Social Dimensions of Collective Identity* [3 microfiches] (Ann Arbor, Mich.: University Microfilms International, 1985), p. 235; Arnon Soffer, "Israeli Arabs and the Palestinian State: Allegiance and Loyalty," *Nativ*, vol. 10, no. 1–2 (1997): 78–81.

3. It is not the only way, to be sure. Switzerland, Belgium, and Canada have multiple "official" languages, with some citizens not being able to speak all of them. But these countries are the exception and not the rule.

4. Formally, Arabic is an official language recognized by the state, but practically, Hebrew is the standard language.

5. Eliezer Ben-Rafael, *Language, Identity, and Social Division: The Case of Israel* (Oxford: Clarendon Press, 1994).

6. The name change has a parallel in the American experience, with U.S. immigration officials finding the given names of certain immigrants difficult to spell or pronounce, and then registering them with more familiar American names.

7. Zvia Walden, "Matchmaking and Not Melting: Direct Language Absorption in Schools," *Hed Hachinuch*, vol. 66, no. 1 (1991): 20–21; Lewis Glinert, "Inside the Language Planner's Head: Tactical Responses to a Mass Migration," *Journal of Multilingual and Multicultural Development*, vol. 16, no. 5 (1995): 351–71.

8. The growing use of English has sparked a backlash among some Israeli academics, who worry that Hebrew will become less important over time among

elites in the country. See Shoshana London Sappir, "Is Hebrew Dying Again?" *Jerusalem Report*, October 10, 2000, pp. 48–49.

9. See Rita Sever, "Anatomy of Immigration, *Aliya*, and Immigrant Absorption in Israel," in Yaakov Kop, ed., *Pluralism in Israel: From Melting Pot to Salad Bowl* (Jerusalem: Center for Social Policy Studies, 2000).

10. The term *Olim* is from the Hebrew root meaning to "ascend," conveying the higher level that Jews attribute to the Land of Israel, nationally and spiritually, as aspired to during the centuries of residence in the Diaspora.

11. Some recent researchers also see in this governmental action a conscious move to create social stratification. See Yiftachel, "Research on Jewish-Arab Relations."

12. Mina Tsemach and Rimona Vizel, *The Adjustment from the Former Soviet Union to Israel, 1990–1995* (Tel Aviv: Machon Mechkar Dachaf, 1996).

13. Olim also receive exemptions from or a combination of loans and grants to pay for customs duties on the importation of household appliances, reduced income tax rates for their first three years in the country, large discounts on pre-kindergarten fees for their children, and free health care for six months unless they find a job earlier.

14. The Yeshivot Hesder—the program that combines religious study and army service—recently objected to the incorporation of women in combat units, claiming that their students could not, on religious grounds, serve in mixed combat units.

15. Of the eighteen-year-old cohort, 75 percent are Jewish (Arabs usually do not serve). Of them, 15 percent do not qualify for the army on medical or other grounds. About 10 percent more are Haredim, who are exempted according to current (political) arrangements.

16. Nathan Glazer and Daniel P. Moynihan, *Beyond the Melting Pot: The Negroes, Puerto Ricans, Jews, Italians, and Irish of New York City* (MIT Press, 1995); Chaim Adler and Nahum Blass, "Inequality in Education in Israel," in Yaakov Kop, ed., *Israel's Social Services 1996* (Jerusalem: Center for Social Policy Studies, 1996), pp. 125–57.

17. The school system of Israel allows parents to choose between state (secular), state-religious, independent, and "other" schools. Most independent schools are run by Haredi for those who consider state-religious schools as not religious enough.

18. In line with Jewish tradition, mainly in Eastern Europe, in Israel a growing number of high-standard boarding schools have emerged, in which academic studies (both religious and secular) are fused with and reinforced by religious practice and cooperative living. This is the *yeshiva*. A similar institution for adolescent girls, which did not exist in Europe, has emerged under the name of *ulpena*.

19. This policy stems from a decision to allow the Arab minority to set educational priorities in accordance with their cultural preferences, with certain basic common elements of the curriculum required throughout the system.

20. Yoram Hazony, *The Jewish States: The Struggle for Israel's Soul* (Basic Books, 2000).

21. A fair number of schools in distressed areas attract supplementary funds from sources other than the Education Ministry.

22. Ministry of Education and Culture, *The Education System in Numbers* (Jerusalem: Ministry of Education and Culture, 1995), p. 45.

23. Data for these comparisons are from Israel's Central Bureau of Statistics.

24. This fact should be viewed in the context of the dropout rate in the religious track schools being greater than that in the (secular) general track schools. This higher dropout rate is a virtual "self-selection" system, whereby fewer weak pupils from the religious track schools choose to sit the matriculation exams.

25. The social security program is especially important to former Soviet Olim, who comprise a higher proportion of the elderly than the rest of the Israeli population.

26. Yosef Katan, "Pluralism and Homogeneity in Israel's Social Services," in Yaakov Kop, ed., *Pluralism in Israel: From Melting Pot to Salad Bowl* (Jerusalem: Center for Social Policy Studies, 2000).

27. See Dov Shinar, "Fifty Years of Media: Pluralism and Sectorialism," in Yaakov Kop, ed., *Pluralism in Israel: From Melting Pot to Salad Bowl* (Jerusalem: Center for Social Policy Studies, 2000); Gady Yatsiv, *The Sectorial Society* (Jerusalem: Bialik Institute, 1999); Dan Caspi, *Media Decentralization: The Case of Israel's Local Newspapers* (New Jersey: Transaction, 1986); Dov Shinar and Mira Moshe, "Proliferation of Channels and Privatization of Broadcasting in Israel: Rhetoric and Reality," in Dan Caspi, ed., *Communications and Democracy in Israel* (Jerusalem: Van Leer Jerusalem Institute and Hakibbutz Hameuhad, 1997), pp. 71–96; Yehiel Limor, "The Stormy Waves of Pirate Radio in Israel," *Kesher,* vol. 19 (1996): 42–57.

28. See Motti Regev, "Popular Music in Israel," in Yaakov Kop, ed., *Pluralism in Israel: From Melting Pot to Salad Bowl* (Jerusalem: Center for Social Policy Studies, 2000), pp. 199–212; Jeff Halper, Edwin Seroussi, and Pamela Squires-Kidron, "Musica Mizrakhit: Ethnicity and Class Culture in Israel," *Popular Music,* vol. 8, no. 2 (1989): 131–42; Edwin Seroussi, *Popular Music in Israel: The First Fifty Years* (Harvard College Library, 1996).

29. *Ha'aretz,* August 12, 2000.

30. Hazony, *The Jewish States.*

Chapter Five

1. The security challenges have, in fact, intensified in recent years. See Uri Ram, *The Changing Agenda of Israeli Sociology: Theory, Ideology, and Identity* (State University of New York Press, 1995); Daniel Bar-Tal, "Societal Beliefs in Israel: From Conflict to Peace," *Palestine-Israel Journal,* vol. 3, no. 1 (1996): 44–50; Ezra

Kopelowitz, "Equality, Multiculturalism, and the Dilemmas of Civility in Israel," *International Journal of Politics, Culture, and Society*, vol. 9, no. 3 (1996): 373–400; Institute of Policy and Strategy, "Assessing Israel's National Strength," first annual Herzliya conference, Herzliya Interdisciplinary Center, December 19–21, 2000.

2. Stephen Sharot, Hanna Ayalon, and Eliezer Ben-Rafael, "Secularization and the Diminishing Decline of Religion," *Review of Religious Research*, vol. 3, no. 27 (1986): 193–207; Stephen Sharot, "Judaism and the Secularization Debate," *Sociological Analysis*, vol. 3, no. 52 (1991): 255–75; Michael Chen and Drora Kfir, "Approaching an Open Society as a Reaction to Social Need," in Rina Shapira and Aryeh Kasher, eds., *Historical, Philosophical, and Social Aspects of Education* (University of Tel Aviv, 1991), pp. 253–73.

3. Meir Horkin, *The Enlistment of Politics, Ethnicity, and Religion and Voting for the Shas Party, 1984–1992* (University of Tel Aviv, Political Science Department, 1993), p. 252; Menachem Friedman, "The Religious and Haredi Communities in Israel after the Twelfth Knesset Elections," *Trends and Processes, Monthly Survey*, vol. 5, no. 36 (1989): 22–36.

4. S. N. Eizenstadt, *Changes in Israeli Society* (Jerusalem: Magnus Press, 1989).

5. The prevailing Israeli expression of this dichotomy is "Right versus Left." However, this distinction has not been applied toward economic matters. Indeed, Likud and Labor governments have hardly differed in their economic policies, in contrast to their strong differences on issues of security and peace. An interesting phenomenon relating to our discussion of pluralism is that lower-income groups tend to vote for the "rightist" Likud and not for the "leftist" Labor Party. This contrasts sharply with Western countries, in which the affluent and upper-middle classes tend to vote for the Republicans in the United States, the Conservatives in Great Britain, and so on, while the low- and lower-middle classes vote for the Democrats, Labor, and the Social Democrats in the United States, the United Kingdom, and Germany, respectively.

6. Ephraim Yaar and Tamar Hermann, "The Peace Index" (University of Tel Aviv, Tami Steinmetz Center for Peace Research, 2001), www.tau.ac.il/peace/Peace_Index/p.index.html.

7. Shevat Weiss, "Summary of the Results of the Fourteenth Elections to the Knesset and Prime Minister—1996" (Tel Aviv: HaKibbutz HaMeuchad, 1997); Asher Arian and Michal Shamir, eds., *The Elections in Israel* (State University of New York Press, 1992).

8. The Arab citizens of Israel appear to be outside the debate. At first glance, one may place them in the dovish camp. However, this is obviously an oversimplification, since one may suspect that their antihawkish views actually reflect solidarity with the Palestinians and the neighboring Arab countries.

9. As one Arab-Israeli, described by the *Economist* as a "radical activist, who runs a union of Arab community associations," was quoted as saying, "We

did not take to the streets in October to demand greater municipal budgets. We took to the streets as part of the Palestinian people" (*Economist,* February 10, 2001, p. 48).

10. See Alizah Shenhar, chairperson, *The Nation and the World: Jewish Culture in a Changing World,* Steering Committee on Jewish Studies in the State Education System (Jerusalem: Ministry of Education, Culture, and Sport, 1994).

11. See Mordechai Kremnitzer, chairperson, *On Being a Citizen: Civics Education for All in Israel,* Steering Committee for Civics Education (Jerusalem: Ministry of Education, Culture, and Sport, 1996).

12. One of the demands that should be presented to the Ultra-Orthodox schools that want state financial support is that they teach the basic tools needed to accomplish this integration into the labor market and general society.

13. Gary Burtless, ed., *Does Money Matter? The Effect of School Resources on School Achievement and Adult Success* (Brookings, 1996).

14. *Ha'aretz,* June 8 and 11, 2000.

15. Yaakov Kop, ed., *Israel's Social Services 1999* (Jerusalem: Center for Social Policy Studies, 1999).

16. See also Robert E. Goodin, Bruce Headley, Ruud Muffels, and Henk-Jan Dirven, *The Real Worlds of Welfare Capitalism* (Cambridge University Press, 1999); and Robert Solow's review of the book: Robert M. Solow, "Welfare: The Cheapest Country," *New York Review of Books,* vol. 47, no. 5 (March 23, 2000): 20–23.

17. Notably, improved measurements in recent years—not described in detail here—make it seem as though the "real" level of inequality was higher in the past. See Shira Klein, "Child Poverty in Israel, 1982–1995," *Economic Quarterly,* Am Oved, vol. 47, no. 4 (December 2000). One doubts that this can provide any consolation in regard to the current situation.

18. See also Lawrence Klein, "Keynesianism Again: Interview with Lawrence Klein," *Challenge,* vol. 44, no. 3 (May–June 2001): 6–16.

19. Itzhak Schnell, *Policy toward Foreign Workers in Israel* (Jerusalem: Center for Social Policy Studies, 2001).

20. See Arthur Hertzberg, "A Small Peace for the Middle East," *Foreign Affairs,* vol. 80 (January–February 2001): 139–47.

21. In fact, community service exists in Israel for religious girls who are not Ultra-Orthodox but still want to serve in a civilian service. This is called the National Service, and participation is voluntary.

Chapter Six

1. U.S. Bureau of the Census, Population Division, *United States Census 2000* (Washington: U.S. Bureau of the Census, 2000).

2. The changing mix of immigrants in the United States is documented in Kenneth Prewitt, "Demography, Diversity, and Democracy," *Brookings Review* (Winter 2002, forthcoming).

3. The United Kingdom is a notable exception in this regard. It has a self-funded pension program that does not face the financial crunch confronting the rest of Western Europe and the United States. See Barry Bosworth and Gary Burtless, eds., *Aging Societies: The Global Dimension* (Brookings, 1998).

4. For a thorough treatment of the funding problems created by aging in Western Europe, Japan, and the United States, see Bosworth and Burtless, *Aging Societies*.

5. Jonathan Coppel, Jean-Christophe Dumont, and Ignazio Visco, "Trends in Immigration and Economic Consequences," OECD Working Paper 284 (Paris: Organization for Economic Cooperation and Development, February 1, 2001).

6. Nicholas Eberstadt, "The Population Implosion," *Foreign Policy,* vol. 123 (March–April 2001): 48.

7. Harry C. Blaney III, "What I See in Europe Isn't Pretty," *Washington Post,* June 3, 2001, p. B5.

8. Eberstadt, "The Population Implosion," p. 49.

9. T. Alexander Aleinikoff and Douglas B. Klusmeyer, eds., *From Migrants to Citizens: Membership in a Changing World* (Washington: Carnegie Endowment for International Peace, 2000).

10. Amitai Etzioni, *The Monochrome Society* (Princeton University Press, 2001), pp. 3–36.

11. See Roberto Suro, *Strangers among Us: How Latin Immigration Is Transforming America* (Alfred A. Knopf, 1998), pp. 303–04.

12. See Mancur Olson, *The Rise and Fall of Nations* (Yale University Press, 1982); Jonathan Rauch, *Demosclerosis: The Silent Killer of American Government* (Times Books, 1994).

13. See Council of Economic Advisers, *Economic Report of the President, 1998* (Government Printing Office, 1998), p. 119.

14. One recent study finds that, controlling for the educational background of the individual, although the decline of "social capital"—measured by the rate of volunteering and membership in group organizations—has been relatively small since the 1950s, the decline is highly correlated with increased diversity of the population and especially with rising income inequality dating from the early 1970s. See Dora L. Costa and Matthew E. Kahn, "Understanding the Decline in Social Capital, 1952–98," NBER Working Paper 8295 (Cambridge, Mass.: National Bureau of Economic Research, May 2001).

15. See Wendy Rahn, "Generations and American National Identity: A Data Essay," prepared for presentation at the Communication in the Future of Democracy Workshop, Annenberg Center, Washington, D.C., April 20, 1998.

16. This policy, implicit for many decades, was adopted formally as part of the 1965 amendments to the Immigration and Nationality Act.

17. This was particularly evident in the early 1970s, less than two decades after the waves of North African immigrants had been resettled under much more spartan conditions. Immigration from the United States was also at a higher level. Since the terms of absorption at the time included exemption from customs taxes on cars and subsidies on housing mortgages, veteran Israelis expressed their resentment in the slogan, "Villa-Volvo benefits."

18. See George J. Borjas, *Heaven's Door: Immigration Policy and the American Economy* (Princeton University Press, 1999).

19. John Micklethwait, "Oh, Say, Can You See? The United States Survey," *Economist*, March 11, 2000, p. 15 of insert following p. 60. See also "Teach English," *Washington Post*, August 9, 2001, p. A18.

20. According to 1997 data, the poverty rate for households headed by immigrants (32 percent) was almost twice as high as that for households headed by native-born Americans (18 percent). Robert J. Samuelson, "Ignoring Immigration," *Washington Post*, May 3, 2000, p. A23.

21. Daniel Golden, "Mixed Signals: No Green Card Means American Education Is a Win-Lose Prospect," *Wall Street Journal*, June 22, 2000, p. A1.

22. Germany requires eighteen months of compulsory military service, while conscientious objectors may serve twenty months of civilian service. Switzerland requires four months of compulsory service, with potential three-week periods of service every two years thereafter.

23. "A National Service Debate," *Wall Street Journal*, May 29, 1981, p. 24.

24. We are not the first to advocate some sort of compulsory service. In the United States, the idea was broached initially during the Depression and has since attracted other supporters through the years, including Representative Pete McLoskey (a decorated Vietnam War veteran in the late 1970s), Charles Moskos and the National Commission on Youth (both in 1980), and authors Richard Danzig and Peter Szanton. Edward Bellamy also offered the concept in a novel published in 1942. See National Commission on Youth, *The Transition of Youth to Adulthood: A Bridge Too Far* (Boulder, Colo.: Westview Press, 1980); Richard Danzig and Peter Szanton, *National Service: What Would It Mean?* (Lexington, Mass.: Lexington Books, 1986); Edward Bellamy, *Looking Backward: 2000–1887* (Modern Library, 1942).

25. The Histadrut is the umbrella organization for most of the workers unions in Israel and is most closely aligned and identified with the Labor Party. Up until the 1970s, the Histadrut was a giant economic enterprise with ownership of companies in diverse fields. It also operated a wide network of social services for its members and, in certain ways, continues to serve the public at large.

26. In the United States, this is an untested proposition, as even the former director of the Bush administration's Faith-Based Initiative acknowledged prior

to his appointment to that position. See John DiIulio, "*The Ambiguous Embrace by Charles L. Glenn*," *Public Interest*, vol. 141 (Fall 2000): 110–15.

27. For contrasting views about the status of American society, whether it is growing apart or moving together, see Gertrude Himmelfarb (suggesting that the country is moving apart) and Alan Wolfe (arguing the opposite). Gertrude Himmelfarb, *One Nation, Two Cultures: A Searching Examination of American Society in the Aftermath of Our Cultural Revolution* (Alfred A. Knopf, 1999); Alan Wolfe, *One Nation, After All: What Middle-Class Americans Really Think about God, Country, Family, Racism, Welfare, Immigration, Homosexuality, Work, the Right, the Left, and Each Other* (Viking, 1998). For a discussion of the role of religion in U.S. politics, see Andrew Kohut and others, *The Diminishing Divide: Religion's Changing Role in American Politics* (Brookings, 2000).

Index